M000251358

Lost Restaurants
OF
JACKSONVILLE

············DOROTHY K. FLETCHER

AMERICAN PALATE

Published by American Palate
A Division of The History Press
Charleston, SC 29403
www.historypress.net

Copyright © 2013 by Dorothy K. Fletcher
All rights reserved

First published 2013
Second printing 2013

Manufactured in the United States

ISBN 978.1.62619.106.8

Library of Congress CIP data applied for.

Notice: The information in this book is true and complete to the best of our knowledge. It is offered without guarantee on the part of the author or The History Press. The author and The History Press disclaim all liability in connection with the use of this book.

All rights reserved. No part of this book may be reproduced or transmitted in any form whatsoever without prior written permission from the publisher except in the case of brief quotations embodied in critical articles and reviews.

Contents

CONTENTS

Preface

When I first considered doing a project on the lost restaurants of Jacksonville, I located a copy of the *Southern Bell, Jacksonville, Fla., Telephone Directory, August 1960*, on the fourth floor of Jacksonville's Main Public Library downtown. I flipped to the restaurant section of the "Yellow Pages" and was amazed that, even then, there were five pages of restaurant listings. Exactly 395 eating establishments were listed in 1960, representing all the eateries of the entire Jacksonville/Duval County area.

As I read through the alphabetical names, I encountered many I did not recognize—like Anderson's Kitchen or Christopher's Pier or Coconut Grove. There were restaurants, however, I did recognize: Le Chateau, the Lobster House, Patti's Italian and American Restaurant and more.

The old phonebook pages also contained familiar advertisements. Strickland's Restaurants had two ads—one was for the Mayport restaurant that featured "THE FINEST SEAFOOD," and the other was for Strickland's Town House, featuring nightly dancing in the "Parisienne Lounge." Fred Abood's Famous Steer Room Restaurant had an ad that touted its "charcoal broiled steaks," and the Lobster House ad featured dancing and cocktails along with "Authentic Polynesian and Cantonese Dishes."

It was a joy to peruse the tattered pages, reliving memories of good times with family and friends. From the first listing, Abood's Steer Room, to the last, Uncle Joe's Place, these restaurants were where parents took their families for Sunday dinner, salesmen entertained their clients, men romanced their sweethearts and teenagers hung out to be cool and really "with it."

This research proved a bit bittersweet, however. So many of the restaurants listed in 1960 are no more. They have been replaced by bigger, more modern franchises, or they simply went away—going out of business or just out of style. It is these restaurants that would be the subject of my searches and the topic of my book.

For almost two hours, I stayed in the library considering my options and my approach until my parking meter was about to expire. It was when I was rushing to my car that I decided that writing a book about the lost restaurants of Jacksonville would be a fun and a meaningful project to take on.

There would be one problem that I had to address. There were simply too many "lost restaurants" for me to cover them all in a book of about thirty thousand words. I was certain to leave out many favorites. Too many restaurants; too little space.

The only thing I could do was to let the places that I remembered best become the basis for my research. I would then make a pilgrimage through the memories of many Jacksonville patrons and restaurant owners and employees. For many days and months after, I buried myself in the microfilm of the *Florida Times-Union*, located on the second floor of the Main Library, and I searched the Internet for whatever restaurant information I could glean.

I altered the table of contents many times as I interviewed people. New restaurants entered the conversations, and I would add them to my list. I also removed many restaurant names that other people did not seem to recall. Hopefully, what is left is a very representative compilation of restaurant histories that exemplifies the best places to eat in the Jacksonville area in earlier times.

As I began researching, I came to another insight: reproducible pictures were going to be difficult to find. It seems that when most people went out to eat, they didn't usually take cameras to record the meal. Since in earlier times there were no iPhones, we didn't often take pictures of ourselves at restaurants. We left the cumbersome cameras, film and flashbulbs at home.

I did think to look through family photo albums to see if I could find any restaurant photographs, but all I found were Christmas morning pictures, Easter clothes pictures and the "grandparents come to town" pictures. These pictures would come to us in a bright orange-yellow three-inch-square booklet from the Cohens Camera Department. In the pictures, we were always smiling, but never were we smiling out in front of a well-known restaurant. And my experience was not at all unusual. I therefore had to rely heavily on postcards, matchbooks, the Florida State Photographic Archives and restaurant promotional materials.

Photograph album for three-inch-square black-and-white family pictures developed in the Cohen Brothers Department Store Camera Department, 1957. *Photo by author.*

Something else happened as I went about my research. As I read the names, phone numbers and addresses, I was quickly reminded that each restaurant represented incredible amounts of effort. In order for these hardworking restaurateurs to earn loyal customers, they had to work late, work weekends and holidays and work through many major family events. Shopping had to be done. Supplies had to be ordered. Onions and celery had to be chopped, potatoes had to be peeled and meat and fish had to be prepped, marinated and cooked. Then, tables had to be set, served and cleaned. And finally, someone had to wash the dishes, while others prepared the place for the next day's business.

I came by some of this restaurant knowledge because I had worked as a HOJO Girl at both the Lane Avenue and Golfair Boulevard Howard Johnson's restaurants during the summers of 1969, 1970 and 1972. I will never forget the backbreaking work that went into making a restaurant function, and I was just a small cog in the whole restaurant mechanism.

So, with all of these thoughts and memories roiling around in my head, I still ran headlong into this "lost restaurant" project. I knew that it would be difficult at times, but it has proven to be a blast revisiting some of the most upscale places of Jacksonville's restaurant history, as well as those mom and pop eateries revered for their cozy surroundings.

Even as I write this, I can almost smell the steaks flaring up on the grill or the pungent smell of lasagna covered with Parmesan cheese. I can hear the clinking of ice in the sweet tea glasses and the soft murmur of happy conversations, and sometimes, if I am lucky, I can hear the sound of a piano or band as I imagine someone swirling across the dance floor. This has proven to be a wonderful project!

PART I
City Core Restaurants

SHORT LINE IN THE CARRIAGE ROOM: MORRISON'S CAFETERIA

In the *Florida Times-Union*, on October 1, 1950, a news article heralded the coming of a Morrison's Cafeteria to a place near Hemming Park. It was to be built at 128–30 West Monroe Street, the site of the demolished YWCA home. The new building was to be designed by Marsh and Saxelbye of Jacksonville, and the building would cost $750,000. It would have two stories and a basement, and S.S. Jacobs Construction Company was awarded the contract to build it.

The article went on to note that the Morrison Cafeteria Company began in Mobile, Alabama, in 1920 with a single cafeteria. By 1950, it had sixteen cafeterias as far west and north as Shreveport, Louisiana; as far east as Savannah, Georgia; and as far south as West Palm Beach, Florida.

J.H. Gibbons, the president of Morrison Cafeteria Company, said, "This new cafeteria [in Jacksonville] will be the largest and most ambitious undertaking of the Morrison Cafeterias. Its size and beauty and the three-quarters of a million dollars to be invested amply demonstrate the faith of our company in the future of Jacksonville. Jacksonville has grown and will continue to grow. The Morrison Cafeteria Company intends to contribute its share towards this growth."

And so began an integral part of Jacksonville's restaurant history: Morrison's Cafeteria near Hemming Park. On any given day in the heart of Jacksonville, as one emerged from shopping at Cohen Brothers Department Store or as one waited for bus connections in the shade of Hemming Park trees, these locally famous words could clearly be heard traveling on the breeze: "Short line in the Carriage Room! No waiting on the Main Floor!"

The powerful voice of the doorman at Morrison's Cafeteria, Captain Charlie McRoy, called to us in a siren-song that has become one of the most enduring restaurant memories of Jacksonville natives and nonnatives alike. Always dressed in white coat, bow tie, dark pants and shiny shoes, Charlie struck quite the pose and left a lasting impression as he ushered us into the aromatic rooms of Morrison's Cafeteria.

Even Elizabeth Edwards, the late wife of the onetime vice presidential hopeful John Edwards, mentioned these very words in her memoire, *Saving Graces: Finding Solace and Strength from Friends and Strangers*. Edwards was part of a military family and had moved quite a bit as a child, but when her father was stationed in Jacksonville, she became part of a collective memory that many of us share. She and her family would eat at Morrison's after Sunday school each week, "beckoned by the intonations of James, the doorman whose warm, 'Come on in, no waiting in the Carriage Room,' drifted across the park and invited us in."

It is interesting that her "James" was mentioned by many people with whom I have spoken as a beloved waiter who carried trays for customers once inside the cafeteria. It is likely that Edwards's recollection is of times when James was filling in for the usual doorman, Captain Charlie.

Charlie McRoy was the official doorman and one of the most iconic parts of Morrison's. He was featured in an article written by Cynthia Parks that appeared in the *Florida Times-Union* on November 16, 1981. Charlie McRoy was at that time seventy-seven years old and living on West Eighteenth Street. He lived in very simple surroundings, and since his retirement after fifty years with Morrison's, he had very little to do except attend church and read his Bible.

According to the article, McRoy started working for Morrison's in 1925. He was still a kid standing on a corner in Montgomery, Alabama, when the cafeteria owner offered him a job. At first, McRoy cut grass at the Morrison's farm in Alabama, and sometimes he washed pots in the cafeteria. There is even mention of his walking "little 'Buddy' Morrison through Hemming Park to see the alligators."

Charlie moved with Morrison's to Jacksonville when a Morrison's opened on Adams Street. When the operation moved to Monroe Street in the early 1950s, Charlie was made headwaiter, and he wore a "big gold-colored No. 1 badge." Then, for the next fifty years, Captain Charlie McRoy crooned to us and brought us to a very happy place for warm, cafeteria-style meals and family togetherness.

Of course, the Morrison's experience was a wonder for little kids. Every imaginable delight was spread before us in long, gleaming counters. Cloth napkins encircled the cleaned and sometimes warm flatware, which would be placed on the tray that slid down the row before a glorious feast. Customers were then asked what they wanted, and cooks and servers saw to it that we got whatever we desired. My parents often had to remind me not to let my "eyes be bigger than my stomach," especially as the mountain of food on my plate grew.

Abbie Young, a retired drug company representative currently living in Lake Mary, Florida, remembered many of her times at Morrison's—that the desserts were very good and the food was replicated well in another Morrison's in the Orlando area but that the best part about the downtown Jacksonville Morrison's was that "I would get to see what I wanted," Young said. That simple sentiment pretty much describes the Morrison's experience of us all.

Almost everyone from the Jacksonville area has a story about Morrison's. Charlie Robertson is a performing songwriter, dubbed "God's personal songwriter" by the late Gamble Rogers, another locally famous performer/ songwriter. Robertson presently lives in St. Augustine, and he has vivid memories of the downtown Morrison's.

"Morrison's was to me, this little kid from Palatka, a sensory overload. Not only was there a mountain of food to be had, but there was quite an eclectic mix of people who went there—people tending to the downtown commerce, crossing over to Cohen's and Ivey's and Furchott's, people from Ortega and moviegoers. It was something else." His memories of Morrison's eventually led Robertson to write a song about it, which is why I sought him out in the first place. The song is entitled "The Ritz Cafe" only because he needed a word with fewer syllables than "Morrison's" to better accommodate the meter of the music. "I did use my poetic license and slapped the truth around a little bit," he said, "but for the most part, I think it captures the essence of Morrison's Cafeteria."

As I listened to Robertson sing on his CD entitled *Witness Protection*, I relived the Morrison's experience as his song immortalized a piece of Jacksonville history that countless other residents share. Using a lively tempo and lyrics with a very simple message, he shows that everyday things really are the stuff of history:

THE RITZ CAFÉ

Chorus: There ain't no line on the Main Floor.
Short line in the Carriage Room.
No line on the Main Floor
Short line in the Carriage Room.
You can eat all you want in a fancy kind of place.
There's steaks, chopped chicken.
You can really feed your face.
Twenty-eight selections on the daily bill o' fare.
Take a tray and park it anywhere.
Don't forget your silverware.
No line on the Main Floor.
Short line in the Carriage Room.

I'm goin' down to that Ritz Café.
Goin' to put that feedbag on.
Give me some home-style turnip greens,
Big ole, greasy, thick filet mignon.
When I get down to that hot spot
Goin' to hear that doorman moan...

Chorus.

Well, I'm going home this mornin,'
That ole Seaboard Railroad Line.
Oh, when I get down to Bay Street,
My poor feet going to be a flyin', high flyin'!
When I reach my destination,
Goin' to hear that doorman cryin'
Just like this...

Chorus.

© *Charles Robertson, 2002,* Witness Protection

Many others were kind enough to share their Morrison's memories with me. Jacksonville resident Melanie Beasley Green is a retired schoolteacher currently working as a substitute teacher in Duval County. She said, "My mother and my father's cousin and I would dress up (even gloves) and go shopping at Cohen's. Then we would go to Morrison's, and I would get to see my favorite waiter, Eddy. I would always get the shrimp salad and a piece of custard pie. Both were the best. Oh yes, and they would let me skip school to do this. Great memory!"

Alvin Brown, retired partner at Simpson Thatcher & Bartlett LLP and now living in New York, said, "When we first moved to Jacksonville in 1956, we lived in an apartment downtown and used to eat at Morrison's downtown often. When we moved, first to an apartment and then a house in Arlington, we started going to the Morrison's on Beach Boulevard. I remember the black waiters in white jackets who carried your trays, although everyone who ate there was white."

D.H. Eaton is a native of Jacksonville and the author of the book *The Osceola Community Club: Sauté and Simmer*. Hers was another great story about Morrison's. "One of my hairstyling salon clients 'stole' for me Morrison's secret recipe for the pineapple congealed salad with the grated cheddar cheese on top," she said. "The restaurant guarded its recipes as though they were gold. She sneaked it for me because I was ape over it. As it turned out, mayonnaise was the ingredient that made it creamy. I had tried whipped cream, sour cream, cream cheese, etc., to no avail. She didn't get caught and went on to retire unscathed after thirty years' service behind the cafeteria line, dishing up meats and seafoods to hungry customers."

Of course, as with all great things, the downtown Morrison's Cafeteria came to an end. In a January 8, 1976 article in the *Florida Times-Union*, it was reported that Morrison's was to "Shut Downtown Unit." The last day at the downtown location was to be Friday, January 9, 1976. Morrison's had already opened a new cafeteria in the Independent Life Building (now the Wells Fargo Building), as well as one "near the top of the Atlantic National Bank Building at the corner of Forsyth and Hogan Street." An Orange Park Mall Morrison's was to open on January 14.

The article went on to note, "The Morrison unit to be closed—opened in 1952—is one of five downtown locations remaining in the Morrison's chain, according to the spokesman [for Morrison's]. It has about 65 employees, all of whom will be offered jobs at the company's suburban cafeterias here, he said." The article later said that "Business at the old Jacksonville Morrison's peaked in the Fifties at 50,000 to 60,000 customers per month, and dwindled since to about half that amount, according to the company. 'It is still making money, but is not up to our requirements.'"

Already the flow of downtown businesses to the suburban locations had begun, signaling the end of an era in Jacksonville history and the demise of such memorable places as Morrison's Cafeteria.

On September 11, 1992, the obituary for Captain Charlie McRoy Sr. ran in the *Times-Union*, saying that Charlie had died on September 3 after a long illness.

In 1999, the last Morrison's in Jacksonville closed. An article by Peralte Paul in the *Florida Times-Union* on July 10 noted, "The Morrison's Cafeteria at 9805 Atlantic Blvd. will shutter its doors tomorrow, marking the end of the chain's decades-long presence in Jacksonville." The article continued, "The Mobile, Ala., chain was purchased for $46 million last year by Piccadilly Cafeterias Inc., a Baton Rouge, La.-based cafeteria chain." Piccadilly Cafeterias were to convert all existing Morrison's locations to Piccadilly's. And that marked the end of Morrison's in Jacksonville.

No matter what, though, I can't help listening for the call of Captain Charlie McRoy any time I walk through Hemming Park. "Short line in the Carriage Room! No waiting on the Main Floor!" still echoes in my head, and I almost hear it as clearly as when I was a child. I'd put money on it that I am not the only person who hears that voice and remembers those days.

THE JEAN RIBAULT ROOM AT SEARS, ROEBUCK & COMPANY

One of the highlights of any Jacksonville childhood was getting to go downtown to shop and have lunch afterward. If my memory serves, the visits were usually at the start of the school year, during Christmas and then near Easter. I recall several times when my family would make our way down to the St. Johns River and to the Sears, Roebuck Department Store for lunch at the Jean Ribault Dining Room.

I don't remember much about the food, if truth be told, but it must have been very good. Whenever I think about Sears, Roebuck & Company and the times we used to go there, I get a pleasant sensation. If I remember correctly, Jacksonville's downtown Sears, which was down by the St. Johns

Jacksonville's Skyline at Night featuring Sears, Roebuck & Company. *Courtesy of the Jacksonville Public Library's Florida Collection.*

River, was one of the biggest Sears in the whole country at that time. For a little girl of the early 1960s, Sears was a most impressive place.

And we were no strangers to Sears, Roebuck & Company. My father used to buy all our appliances there—refrigerators, washing machines, lawn mowers and more. He would even joke that he was going to owe Sears fifty dollars per month for the rest of his life, so he might as well give it all his business.

For me, the most memorable part of the Sears dining experience was the actual dining room, named for the monumental thirty-one- by eight-foot depiction of Jean Ribault's arrival on the shores of the St. Johns River. This magnificent canvas hung on the wall behind the long buffet counter. As we collected our peas, carrots, roast beef and desserts, we gazed at scantily clad Timacua natives welcoming to the New World a group of sixteenth-century French soldiers and colonists. A bountiful feast of native foods was set out for the Europeans and a tiny rendering of Fort Caroline glistened in the background.

As a little kid, I was most impressed with the life-size people in a painting that was almost as large as the wall of my living room. I would gaze at the beautifully rendered composition of people interacting in a lush, tropical setting as we made our way down the food line.

Ribault's Landing, a painting by Lee Adams. *Courtesy of the City of Jacksonville.*

Imagine my surprise and delight when, not a year ago, I turned a corner on the fourth floor of the Jacksonville's Main Library, and there on the wall, near the Florida Room, was the exact same magnificent painting from my childhood: *Ribault's Landing* (1959) by Lee Adams. I felt as if I had somehow slipped back a number of decades into my childhood, although the painting did not seem as big as I remembered.

Emily Lisska, executive director of the Jacksonville Historical Society, who was also largely instrumental in the restoration of it, has some interesting memories of this painting. She said, "The place [Jean Ribault Room] was off-limits to me, although I do remember peering into the room and thinking I was seeing very extraordinary wallpaper. My lunch was usually taken at a saloon with wooden floors on Bay Street that my grandmother had given me directions to—the name escapes me. I seemed to be the only young person there—being about eleven or twelve, and I was there having lunch with all the businessmen in their business suits. And no ladies. No one ever asked me to leave, though, and I never had any problems there."

It is quite an extraordinary story that concerns the painting and its travels since the days my parents would treat us to lunch at Sears or when Emily Lisska would peek through the restaurant doors. According to an article in the *Florida Times-Union* from December 2, 2000, the Sears Building on Bay

Street was closed in 1981, so the painting was rolled up and stored in the basement of Lee High School. There it lay until the mid-1990s, when City Councilman Jim Overton wanted to find the painting and have it placed in the newly renovated city hall.

Jim Draper, the owner of Pedestrian Gallery, coordinated the restoration of a badly damaged canvas. In the article, Draper said, "When the Sears building was torn down, they rolled the painting up and put it in this kind of weird wooden box they had made just to store it…When we removed the painting from the box and unrolled it, what we found was pretty much garbage…Oh, there were whole areas where the roaches had just eaten the paint completely off."

The article goes on to say that Marilyn Linder, a freelance painter and restorer, came up from Gainesville three days a week to assist in restoration. While Linder was busy repairing the painting, Jane Condon, who eventually became the principal of LaVilla School of the Arts, was able to successfully lobby to have the painting displayed in her school.

The painting was then set to be restored yet again so that it could be part of Jacksonville's 450th birthday and the anniversary of Ribault's arrival in north Florida.

The plaque next to the painting reads:

Ribault's Landing by Lee Adams
Mixed Media on Canvas
Restored in 2000 and 2012 by Jim Draper

The 2012 restoration of Ribault's Landing was made possible through the support of the Cultural Council of Greater Jacksonville and the following generous contributors:

Saft America
Helen Lane Jess and Brewster J. Durkee Foundation
Emily and Lawrence Lisska
Martha Barrett
Lynn Corley
Paul M. Harden
JEA
The Hon. James N. Overton
Michelle A. Barth

The City of Jacksonville also thanks the Duval County School Board, the Jacksonville Historical Society, the Jacksonville Public Library and Joanelle Mulrain for their work on behalf of this important project.

Then, according to a message from Mayor Alvin Brown on the City of Jacksonville's website (www.coj.net) on May 1, 2012, at 5:00 p.m., as part of the 450th anniversary of Ribault's landing in north Florida, the mural was permanently installed on the wall near the Florida Room on the Fourth Floor of the Downtown Public Library. And that is how I came to see it—again.

Mention of the artist in the 2002 *Times-Union* article was minimal. It said only that the artist was internationally known and that he and his wife had died in a car crash in 1971. An article about the accident ran in the *Times-Union* on November 17, 1971. The fatal accident occurred on Blanding Boulevard and Plymouth Street at 9:15 p.m. Their obituaries, which ran a few days later, filled in many details of their lives. Lee Adams was forty-nine at the time of his death, and his wife, Mildred Stockton Adams, was forty-four. They were both lifelong residents of Jacksonville, and they lived in Mandarin.

Lee had attended Rollins College and the University of North Carolina and held a degree in biology. Apparently, it was during this time that he became known for his painting of natural subjects. Later, he began to exhibit his works in the Audubon House, the Los Angeles County Museum, the New York Botanical Gardens, Phi Beta Kappa Memorial House and many other places throughout the United States. His work was also included in private collections of famous people—Mrs. Dwight D. Eisenhower, Russell Firestone, Gilbert Grosvenor, John H. Baker and others.

Mildred Stockton Adams had majored in art and sculpture at Rollins College and had served as the chairman of the Air Pollution Control Board of Jacksonville during its first year, 1968. Mr. and Mrs. Adams were survived by three daughters.

There is something terribly poignant about reading the details of the life and death of a person whose work had so influenced the lives of so many citizens of Jacksonville—those who ate their lunches at the Jean Ribault Room at the Sears, Roebuck way back when, those students and teachers who experienced it at LaVilla School of the Arts and those of us who now get to see it at the Main Library of Jacksonville Public Library at 303 North Laura Street.

The vibrant colors of the paints and powerful structural designs of the large canvas give dignity to a seminal moment in our Jacksonville history. We can all be proud that so many individuals came together to preserve the work of such a talented Jacksonville native son whose vision was to preserve our earliest recorded historical event. Such reverence for a treasure that could have gone to the landfill is remarkable. How thankful we should be that such forward-thinking citizens came to the rescue.

THE STEER ROOM

I was not aware of it until I began writing this book, but every time I have wandered the produce stalls of the present-day farmers' market with my grandchildren, I was within one hundred yards of the location of Joe Adeeb's Steer Room, which later became Sandy's Steer Room. The Steer Room was located at the foot of the Beaver Street viaduct and was very much a part of the Jacksonville consciousness. I am told that the farmers' market and the old restaurant have overlapping foundations.

I may never have eaten at the Steer Room, but that does not mean I was unaware of it. My parents had been there often and talked of it quite

Interior of the Steer Room. *Courtesy of the Jacksonville Public Library's Florida Collection.*

frequently. Many of my friends remember it as well. It was a place where entertaining clients was common, and as I recall, if you wanted a wonderful steak, *this* was the place to go.

Joe Adeeb, who opened the restaurant in 1950, was the progenitor of a restaurant dynasty that still has members running restaurants today. Barry Adeeb, who had for many years operated the Sea Turtle and who now runs the Beaches Diners, is the grandson of Joe Adeeb, so it is easy to see that the restaurant business is in the bloodline of this hardworking restaurant family.

In an article in the *Jacksonville Journal's* last edition, which ran on October 28, 1988, Joyce Phelps wrote, as her final column, very poignant reviews of restaurants that had also gone the way of the *Jacksonville Journal*—out of business. She highlighted the histories of many of Jacksonville's most legendary restaurants. The article was entitled "Restaurants Can Empathize with Journal Plight," and it was like a who's who list of restaurants that had flourished and then passed into oblivion.

Phelps said in the article that by 1956, when Joe Adeeb still owned it, the Steer Room was named one the best twenty-five steakhouses in

America. The next owner was Fred Abood, and he kept up the quality tradition for the next sixteen years. Along with excellent service, the Steer Room had famously wonderful cuts of beef, as well as its "White Cargo" after-dinner drink made with ice cream and liqueurs. Many still remember the White Cargo.

During the time Fred Abood was the owner, he commissioned a very nice advertising card to promote the business. On the front of the card was a photograph of the interior of the restaurant, and on the back was the following copy certainly meant to whet appetites: "2000 years ago, the Phoenicians broiled whole steers over beds of glowing charcoal. The Phoenicians knew what was cooking, even then, but Fred Abood gives the secret of ancients, PLUS, in his famous STEER ROOM, where thick, juicy, well aged steaks of prime western beef are served in an atmosphere designed to complete the gourmet's enjoyment in eating them...The STEER ROOM is adequately but softly lighted, cypress paneled, air conditioned of course. Sound proofed except for the smacking of lips and contented conversation between well fed customers. The Service? Naturally, of the same excellence as the food."

There was also a small side-bar on the card that read, "Fred Abood's STEER ROOM is the rendezvous of customer and client, old friends well met or you and your favorite date. A STEER ROOM Steak is a sure way to any man or woman's heart."

This card certainly provided vital information for Jacksonville patrons to consider—including décor, lighting and air conditioning—all meant to enhance the dining experience. And if my parents' comments were accurate, the experience at the Steer Room was mighty fine.

The final *Jacksonville Journal* article went on to report that Fred Abood sold the Steer Room to Sanford "Sandy" Edwards, and the name was changed to Sandy's Steer Room. According to a menu from the Sandy's Steer Room days, one could get a boneless strip sirloin dinner for $6.50. "Steak for Two" was "Carved at your table," and it cost $6.00 per person. Prime rib "au jus" was $5.25, and for the same price, one could have calves liver served with onion rings.

The *Jacksonville Journal* article also noted that in 1977, Sandy's Steer Room burned to the ground and "Sandy Edwards and golfer/developer Gary Holmes served 4 months in jail for charges related to the fire." The restaurant was never rebuilt.

It is a sad commentary that such a happy place could have fallen on such dark times, but that's what happened. It cannot, however, diminish the memories of those who enjoyed meals there, and it certainly falls pleasantly on my mind every time I wander the aisles of the farmers' market on Beaver Street looking for fresh produce.

Ivory's Chili Parlor and Barbeque

In the area that is now called LaVilla, at the corner of West Ashley and Jefferson Streets (at 702 West Ashley Street, to be precise), there was once a thriving restaurant that not only served chili and barbeque but also some of the best soul food in Jacksonville.

Ivory's Chili Parlor and Barbeque was owned and operated by Ivory Abraham Manuel and his wife, Lillie Mae Choice Manuel. Ivory was born on August 4, 1904, in Lamont, Florida. He had five brothers and six sisters, and when he was about fifteen, he headed for Jacksonville, where he met Lillie Mae Choice. Lillie Mae was born on October 26, 1911, in Greenville, Florida, and she had three brothers and four sisters. Lillie Mae and Ivory met in Jacksonville, but their courtship remained somewhat a mystery. In earlier times, such details were never really discussed with the children, those things being private, so all we know for certain was that they married in Jacksonville.

In 1946, after having worked at Key's Chili Parlor on Forsyth Street for several years during the war, Ivory opened his own restaurant in the old New Deal Cab Company. From that time forward, the family referred to their establishment as "the shop." It had about six booths and a counter with about the same number of stools, and if there were ever a family concern, then this would have to be it.

Ivory's Chili Parlor was in a very busy location. Across Ashley Street was the Strand Theater, and across Jefferson Street there was a hot dog stand and the Lenape Bar. This location meant that Ivory's would open at 11:00 a.m. and serve lunch to customers who worked at the post office and the train station. Truck drivers, cleaners and deliverymen were also part of the regular clientele. Dinner customers mostly came from the neighborhood, and the restaurant stayed open late to serve any of the moviegoers who might be hungry when the theater let out. It was a grueling schedule for the hardworking owners.

I sat down with Barbara Manuel Reddick, a retired teacher with thirty-five years of service in the Duval County School System, and her brother, Kenneth

Above: The staff of Ivory's Chili Parlor and Barbeque. *Courtesy of Ken Manuel and Barbara Manuel Reddick.*

Left: Lillie Mae Choice Manuel. *Courtesy of Ken Manuel and Barbara Manuel Reddick.*

LOST RESTAURANTS OF JACKSONVILLE

Leon Manuel, formerly a regional superintendent and currently an associate director of Florida SACS CASI, AdvancED Florida. These extraordinary people are two of the three children of Ivory and Lillie Mae Manuel. They owe much of who they are to Ivory's Chili Parlor and Barbeque and to the example that their hardworking parents showed them.

Barbara said that she has early memories of leaving school at Matthew Gilbert, from which she would graduate in 1959, taking the no. 12 Florida bus and transferring to the no. 20 Beaver bus in order to work in "the shop." She could even recall the shop's old phone number, 49-123, and that Chesterfield cigarette poster ads were placed in all the windows.

"My job then," Reddick said, "was to peel potatoes, chop celery and shell peas, whatever. Why, when I got married, even my husband helped by washing dishes." When I asked if she had any enduring memory she would want to share, she became very thoughtful and then said, "I didn't realize how safe I was and how much my parents impressed in me the values that I have today. I didn't give them credit for being great entrepreneurs."

Kenneth then added, "My parents and the rest of us never thought of ourselves as entrepreneurs. But our corporate income meant that we *all* worked, and we contributed to *all* the family. We were not only able to get by, but my sister, seven cousins and I could afford to go all the way through college. That was certainly something."

Back in the day of Ivory's Chili Parlor and Barbeque, the prices were unbelievably low, so the volume must have been considerable for them to have helped so many family members along. The prices for the dishes had to be memorized since there were no printed menus. A printed list didn't come into existence until someone in the family typed it up for a Manuel/Choice family reunion memory book many years later.

There was fried chicken, fried fish, smothered pork chops and liver dinners at just $0.78. The beef stew, hog maws, neck bones, pig feet, pig's ears, salmon croquettes and chitterlings were just $0.67. A slab of ribs was $2.10 and the most expensive item on the list. A barbeque sandwich was $0.52, T-bone steak was $1.75 and a bowl of the signature Ivory's Chili was only $0.26 (it was $0.52 if you added hot tamales to the order). Sunday dinners included baked chicken with cornbread dressing, roast beef and baked ham, each platter-sized plate costing just $0.95.

All manner of fresh vegetables was available and served in soup bowls: green beans, lima beans, squash, okra, corn and tomatoes. They bought ready-made fruit and sweet potato pies from a Mr. Norris, the pie man, but they made their own hoecakes and cornbread.

Kenneth Manuel
and Barbara Manuel
Reddick. *Photo by author.*

The Manuel siblings mentioned often how different the world was back then. Barbara could take the bus all over town—from Myrtle Avenue to Kings Street to Edward Waters College—and she and her parents never thought a thing about it. Kenneth remembered being sent with fifty dollars to the neighborhood bar to get change for the restaurant. His parents didn't use banks. (They never had a bank account, never had a car and never had stocks or bond investments.) Kenneth would, in full view of everyone in the bar, put the change in his pockets and then leave and walk down the street, and no one ever bothered him or tried to rob him.

There was such a glow of pride when Barbara and Kenneth talked about their parents and the days they spent at Ivory's Chili Parlor and Barbeque. Kenneth said that one of the greatest lessons that he learned from his time working at his family's restaurant was "how to interact with people." He went on to say, "Even when people came in who had had too much to drink, we were to treat them with dignity and respect."

Such wisdom explains how Ivory's Chili Parlor and Barbeque remained such a powerful influence in the Manuel/Choice families, in the LaVilla neighborhood and in the history of Jacksonville's restaurants.

BERNEY'S RESTAURANT, JENKS RESTAURANT AND KEY'S CHILI PARLOR

These three downtown restaurants are among those of which I have absolutely no firsthand knowledge. I never went to these places for one reason or another, but enough people remember them that they needed to be included in this collection.

Joyce Phelps began her final column for the *Jacksonville Journal*, on October 28, 1988, with a bit on Berney's Restaurant, saying that "everybody who was anybody went" to Berney's. It was a restaurant on Adams Street opened by Bernard Berney and Gus Seligman on St. Patrick's Day in 1927. That is probably why Bernard chose to become the famous "Man in Green," even though he was not Irish (he was actually a Russian Jewish immigrant).

In 1932, Berney had bought out his partner and for forty years ran a business where everything was green—menus, napkins, tablecloths, Berney's suits and even the clothes of his little dog, Peggy. Berney was even featured in Ripley's Believe It or Not! for being the "Man in Green."

According to the *Journal* article, when Berney retired, he sold the business to Danville Vickery, who had been with Berney's Restaurant for thirty years. Without the "Man in Green," though, the establishment didn't last long. After many other businesses tried to make a go of it at that location, the place was finally vacated.

THE SECOND SPOT is Jenks. It was located at 201 Main Street, and it bragged in ads that "Our Food is Good, Our Prices Reasonable." It is another restaurant that people mention often. Jenks Restaurant closed down in 1945, five years before I was even born. Still, it was very much a part of the fabric of restaurant life for earlier generations of Jacksonville citizens.

Postcard of Berney's Restaurant. *Courtesy of the Jacksonville Public Library's Florida Collection.*

Buddy Ross, retired finance and budget control supervisor for the Department of Public Works of Florida, was just a little boy back in the early '30s. His father was a policeman who directed traffic at Main and Bay Street, Main and Forsyth Street and Main and Adams Street. He occasionally walked a beat at night in downtown Jacksonville.

When his father took the night shift, he would walk from store to store and restaurant to restaurant, checking to be sure that the locks were secure and that the businesses were safe. Because the shop owners were grateful for the police presence, they were often generous with their goods and services.

Buddy's father was not one to take advantage of this gratitude. Once a month, when he took Buddy downtown on Saturday so that Buddy could go to the movies, Harry Howell, one of the owners of Jenks Restaurant, insisted on serving the little boy a big steak when the father and son were walking home.

"Come on in and let's give the boy a steak," Buddy said, mimicking Mr. Howell's insistent tone when Buddy's father would decline to take him up on his offer. "'Won't cost you anything!' he'd say. And so when my father said, 'All right,' my eyes would get so big. Imagine. Steak!"

According to a May 7, 1975 article in the *Florida Times-Union* by Judge May, Jenks Restaurant was opened in 1911, when Thomas W. Jenks from

Postcard of interior of Jenks Restaurant. *Courtesy of the Jacksonville Public Library's Florida Collection.*

Hamilton, Ontario, read a brochure about Jacksonville and decided to come here to escape the Canadian winters. He met Harry Howell, and they opened a restaurant on Main Street between Forsyth and Bay, opposite Furchott's.

In the article, one of the people interviewed, a Mrs. Josephine Clarke, had been a waitress at Jenks for seventeen years, from 1928 until 1934. She recalled that many political and civic leaders often ate at Jenks. Even Mayor John Alsop, for whom the Main Street bridge is named, was a regular at Jenks. Motion picture stars and national political figures dined there, as did juries from the circuit and criminal courts. Jurors were shown to a private room, the Blue Room, as a bailiff monitored them and made sure that there was no contact with anyone not on the jury. Mrs. Clark said, "We couldn't talk to them, only take their orders."

When Furchott's decided to move to Adams and Hogan, Jenks Restaurant moved one block north on the east side of Main between Forsyth and Adams. Eventually, the partnership between Jenks and Howell dissolved, and Mr. Jenks moved the restaurant to the old Board of Trade Building at the east corner of Main and Adams. After a major remodeling, Jenks reopened in 1937. Tom's brother, Garnet Jenks, supervised kitchen operations, while Tom ran the dining room.

Just recently, I was sent a YouTube clip over Facebook that proved how much a part of Jacksonville Jenks was. The video was called "Vintage Florida Films—1942—Part One." The informational copy said that the film was found at a garage sale and was purchased by Tim Peddy in San Jose, California. No one is sure who was filming the trip from New York to Jacksonville and then to Pensacola in 1942. The California Pioneers of Santa Clara County digitized the film.

As I watched the computer screen, I was thrilled when all of a sudden, there was a night shot of Jacksonville's downtown. The name "Jenks" beamed in a huge, bright-green neon sign over the entrance. Yellow light bulbs pulsed beneath the name, and "Open All Night" was backlit with bright white light. I had an eerie sensation of being present in a totally different time—standing right outside waiting to go to supper in a place that exists only in history for me. Sadly, Jenks closed just before Labor Day in 1945, just three years after the footage of the YouTube video was shot.

THE FINAL RESTAURANT is Key's Chili Parlor, the restaurant where Ivory Manuel got his start making chili before he opened his own chili place. It was the oldest restaurant in Jacksonville when it closed its doors in 1981. In an article in the *Florida Times-Union* from April 29, 1981, "Neighbor" editorial director Joe Smedley wrote that the restaurant had opened on Forsyth Street in 1910 with a menu that didn't include chili. T.M. Key had moved his successful restaurant from Louisville, Kentucky, where it had been in operation since 1892. In Jacksonville, Key had hired a Mexican cook who had been stranded in Jacksonville, and the cook "begged Key to try his specialty, chili and tamales." The chili and tamales were so good that Keys penciled them onto the menu, and before long, "chili and tamales dominated the menu and finally the restaurant changed its image to Mexican."

Over the years, the restaurant moved many times—from Forsyth to Bay, Cedar, Pearl and back to Forsyth. According to the article, Key opened a second store on Main between Ashley and Beaver.

Charlie Robertson, the songwriter who wrote the song about Morrison's Cafeteria, had a rather unflattering comment to share about Key's Chili Parlor. He said that he often laughed when he and his parents went there, since the owners proudly displayed their "Fair" health rating near the cash register. "I'm not sure I'd be so forthcoming with that information," he laughed, "but it didn't seem to hurt business any since it was always packed."

Sharon Gould shared a wonderful note about Key's Chili Parlor in her *Times-Union* column "Then and Now" on July 30, 1967. She mentioned that it was "a great democratizer; Senators ate there and so did vagrants; cab drivers parked their vehicles outside and streetcar motormen, on a break from their trolleying, ordered a quick snack; *Times-Union* newsboys ambled in for a bite and *Times-Union* editor-in-chief W.M. Ball often sat at the counter ladling down a bowl of the hot stuff."

Gould later went on to say in her column that "many early film 'names' were seen with their elbows on Mr. Key's marble counter; Oliver Hardy's healthy appetite was among those that were satisfied by a thick-sauced bowlful."

In 1931, Gould reported that Key sold out. "Half interest went to his nephew, William K. Webb and the other half was purchased by Mrs. Ted Smotherman, a widow of the long-time city recorder. The present owner [1967], Roger Smotherman, her son, got acquainted with the chili business when he was 12 years old. Roger and Helen Smotherman ran the parlor using the same recipe T.M. Key learned from the stranded Mexican cook."

Gould continued, "'Folks kept saying the chili was good enough to sell on the general market, so we decided to try it' [said Roger Smotherman]. At first the Smothermans opened a canning plant in the kitchen of the parlor, then in 1949, they opened a larger facility which now distributes Key's Chili and related products through grocery store outlets in the area."

Gould ended the piece with an explanation of what "Chili and Two" meant. It stands for a bowl of chili and two hot tamales. And many an old-timer would say, "I remember when you could get chili and two for $.15 and a glass of buttermilk for a nickel."

Now, if you have a hankering for a bowl of Key's Chili, you must go to a local grocery store. There in the canned meat section, you'll find Key's Chili, which is distributed by Blue Ribbon Foods. The Smotherman family no longer owns the canning operation, but it is an integral part of Jacksonville's restaurant history.

Worman's, Leb's and Waldz Delicatessens

If I were to close my eyes and think about Worman's Delicatessen, I would certainly revisit the wonderful flavor combinations of their famous Reuben sandwich, which is what I always ordered when I went there. The corned beef, sauerkraut, Swiss cheese and grilled rye bread were just the perfect combination, and when it was served with a crisp deli pickle and their special potato salad, I would be beside myself!

Many other people remember Worman's, like Jacksonville native Nancy Blackmer. "Many years ago, I lived in a garage apartment right across the street from Worman's deli in San Marco, and I thought I had died and gone to heaven. Sunday morning, I would get up and put the coffee on and then go across the street to get the Sunday paper and a cheese Danish, still my favorite when indulging. I would walk back across the street and have my coffee, Danish and read the paper. Also, I can almost taste those delicious dill pickles served with a hot pastrami sandwich. Yum!"

Worman's is still one of Jacksonville's more iconic eating establishments. As with many restaurants, it was a family-owned and family-run operation from its earliest days. In a May 6, 2005 article in *Downtown This Week* written by Amy Limbert, she noted that Worman's opened as a bakery on Duval Street back in 1923. This was after Rose and Sam Worman saw an ad for a Jacksonville bakery that included a truck, machinery and display cases. They paid $350 and moved from New York to Jacksonville. Their children, Pearl and Morris, were born shortly after.

An August 7, 2009 article published in the *Florida Times-Union* and written by Kevin Turner noted that the bakery was called the New York Star Bakery. Then, in 1935, the family moved to Daytona and came back to Jacksonville in 1939, where they opened Worman's Delicatessen on Broad Street.

In *Downtown This Week*, Lambert said that Worman's opened a second location in San Marco, where European Street is now located. The San Marco location closed in 1994 and moved to Lakewood shopping center. This closed in 2000.

Pearl Worman Lebowitz-Sederbaum and her brother, Morris Worman, were the second generation of the Worman family to run the deli, and the third generation included each of their sons.

While the Broad Street location maintained itself, the family waited for the new courthouse to open, bringing with it all the people the justice system would include—lawyers, clients, judges, juries and spectators. Unfortunately, it became harder and harder to make a profit as the opening of the courthouse was delayed over and over again. The family was finally forced to close the business in August 2009. On August 16, 2012, after seven decades, the century-old building was demolished.

I WOULD BE REMISS if I didn't mention another locally famous downtown deli: Leb's. According to the article by Joyce Phelps in the last issue of the *Jacksonville Journal*, Leb's was in its day "the closest thing to New York deli-style eating in Jacksonville." It opened its doors on West Adams Street in 1946 and very soon became extremely popular. One could get corned beef on rye, pastrami, oysters on the half-shell, cheese blintzes, sweet-and-sour Hungarian-style cabbage and cheesecakes. They also made wonderful breads—rye, pumpernickel, egg rolls, onion rolls and five types of bagels.

Loretta Sheil Gangaware Glenn told me, "I used to meet my father there [at Leb's] for lunch on Fridays when I had my first job at Furchgott's. I loved their Manhattan clam chowder."

Leb's closed in 1969, and in the early '80s, it reopened in the Baymeadows area. Here it was not successful and went quietly into oblivion without much fanfare.

ONE LAST DELI needs to be mentioned to round out the list: Waldz. Back in the '40s, when he was on leave during World War II, Edward Hodz married a girl named Elisabeth (Ellie). Not long after, Edward's younger sister, Marilyn, married Stuart Walters. They all decided to go to Jacksonville because Eddie's two other sisters and their families were already living here. Stuart, who had worked for a restaurant chain in New York, thought that a deli-type of restaurant would be good for Jacksonville.

When they opened their business, they took the "wal" from Mr. Walters's name and the "dz" from Mr. Hodz's name, and Waldz Delicatessen and Bakery was born. This authentic New York–style deli was first nestled in a storefront on University Boulevard in Arlington, about three blocks from the Town and County Shopping Center in Arlington. For many years, this haven of rye bread, pastrami, pickles and to-die-for cheesecake was a gathering place for kids from Terry Parker and students from Jacksonville University who were fed up with the college's food plan.

According to Marshall Hodz, the son of Mr. Hodz and a retired baker and restaurateur himself, the families came to Jacksonville from Elmont, Long Island, in 1964. It was here in Jacksonville that they came up with the combination name, and it seems to have served them very well. They operated their deli in the storefront until they learned that the post office was closing in the Town and Country Shopping Center. Since they needed more room, they moved to the shopping center as soon as they could. They went from 60 seats to about 150.

Hodz said, "In the beginning, Arlington was like a hub in Jacksonville— it was close to downtown and happening places like the Thunderbird. JU students used us as their home away from home, coming here five nights a week. As a matter of fact, some of these students were from my old hometown, and I even knew their brothers and sisters."

"Eventually, like from the late '60s to the early '80s, we began to shift from a restaurant to bakery—where more was going out the back door instead of coming in the front door," he continued. "Arlington had begun to change. The Thunderbird had lost its luster, and the neighborhoods were changing. So was our clientele. In 1985, we closed the restaurant, but we kept the bakery going. By the late '90s, we were the largest independent wholesale bakery in the area. We sold baked goods to all kinds of restaurants—the Green Turtle, all the country clubs, the Loop, the Tree Steak House, Firehouse Subs, Steak N Ale, Victoria Station, Annie Tiques, you name it. We even sold to Flowers Bakery and Dandee Foods. We had thirty employees who were bakers and boxers and we had three trucks, and we ran the place twenty-four hours a day."

He concluded, saying, "We even were asked to submit our recipe for cheesecake to *Gourmet* magazine, but we declined. We were still trying to build our business and didn't want to give our recipe away. I suppose if they asked us today, I might consider it, though."

Alvin Brown, who now lives in New York, has very fond memories of this place and the people who ran it. "Waldz Delicatessen at Town and Country was for years as much a community center as it was a restaurant. The cheesecake was *amazing*! Many times, my parents would go there after going to the movies. They would get the cheesecake, some coffee and then 'kibitz' with the sisters."

Progress may be necessary and desirable. It is not always kind, however. Those of us who remember superior Reuben and hot pastrami sandwiches served with crisp Kosher pickles really miss places like Worman's, Leb's and Waldz. And someday, if we are lucky, we might just find the special recipe for cheesecake in *Gourmet* magazine that will remind us of Jacksonville days and delis gone by.

THE EMBERS RESTAURANT

Back during a time when all the world was focused on outer space and astronauts were as important to us as movie stars and political figures,

Jacksonville became a very modern city indeed when it opened a revolutionary restaurant—one that rotated on top of a building. The Embers Restaurant was not only a restaurant, but it was also an extraordinary piece of engineering.

In the *Florida Times-Union* on November 7, 1963, a news article noted that Robert H. Jacobs, developer of the downtown center, announced that the Embers Inc., a national restaurant chain, was to be opened on the top of floor of the Universal Marion Building, at 25 West Church Street. Alen Glen, president of the restaurant firm, said that the new restaurant would be called the Embers and that Eric D. Maier of New York City had been appointed manager.

The article reported that the restaurant would "begin operation in early December and will be open for lunch and dinner. The dining room was built on a turntable, which permits the entire floor to revolve and gives the diners a view of the city from its 20th-floor location."

The Embers was truly a place of space-age wonder. The cuisine was elegant, and diners were able to enjoy a panorama of the city while they ate. Everyone had to give the place a try, and countless of us came to enjoy the magic.

Sandy Gould of the *Florida Times-Union* certainly agreed with this assessment in an article she wrote for the *Sunday Magazine*, published on December 26, 1966. According to her, the Embers restaurant was "[l]ike a sleek glassed-in spaceship—slowly spinning," and that certainly was an apt description, as anyone can attest who has ever dined there.

Gould went on to describe what could be seen of the city as the restaurant silently rotated a full 360 degrees. First, there were "bright clad city glows, trimmed in the season's reds and greens." Then, "the dark layers of the unfinished Gulf Life Building [that] slice a silhouette against the skyline." Then followed the "multi-hued candycane of the WJXT tower" and the "blue coverlet of residential Jacksonville," and finally, "the Mathews Bridge is like a fairyspan—disembodied lights on the far horizon."

Gould's article goes on to tell about the owner, Carl Holmquist, who grew up in Sweden, where he got his start in the food industry by peeling potatoes and stoking the coal oven in a restaurant in his hometown. After he was drafted into the ski troops and served his tour of duty, he worked in Stockholm. He then worked in the restaurant of the Hotel de Crillon in Paris. His work with the Swedish-American Line brought him to the States. When he bought the Embers, some years after it had opened, he brought tremendous experience and talent with him.

The Universal Marion Building. *Courtesy of the Jacksonville Public Library's Florida Collection.*

Postcard of the interior of the Embers Restaurant. *Courtesy of the Jacksonville Public Library's Florida Collection.*

Several articles about the Embers follow in the *Florida Times-Union.* On November 22, 1965, an interview with Holmquist highlighted some of the world-class dishes offered at the Embers: veal noisettes, chasseur, beef roulade à la Marion, and veal cutlet cordon bleu. There was also mention of the seafood fare: broiled Danish lobster tails, South African rock lobster tails, Danish rainbow trout stuffed with crabmeat and mushrooms and seafood kebobs.

And all of this was being prepared and served to a clientele certain to be dazzled by the city panorama that slowly inched its way past their view. And if that were not enough to make the night special, live piano music was provided by Lou Corbin from 7:00 p.m. to 11:30 p.m. weekdays and from 7:00 p.m. until 12:20 a.m. on weekends.

Jacksonville resident Stephanie Robertson Feria, a graphic designer for Florida Blue, remembered the Embers very well. "I loved that place. My parents took me there for my sixteenth birthday, and my dad ordered alcoholic drinks for the adults and a Shirley Temple for me. Well, when the drinks came, everybody was talking and drinking, and when I tasted my drink, *bam.* It wasn't a Shirley Temple at all. I whispered to my dad and told him. He said, 'Enjoy!' Now I know why the waitress winked and said, 'Happy Birthday.' Fun times!"

View of Jacksonville as seen from the space that once held the Embers Restaurant. *Photo by author.*

D.H. Eaton, a native resident and author of the novel *The Osceola Community Club*, remembered the Embers very well and had this to say about it. "You may recall that it [the Embers] was atop the Universal Marion building, near where Ivey's Department Store was also located. You may also recall that it was a revolving restaurant. I remember that it came along at the time of the great 'flaming foods' craze that swept the nation; seems the French word often used on such menus was 'flambé.' I know I was 'flambéed' there, where both entrée and dessert were fired up fancifully."

Eaton also shared one of her teenaged experiences with me. "In my own experience, at age sixteen in 1965, I took a fun job as a 'fashion show director' for Sarah Coventry costume jewelry and staged home parties at ladies' homes, of course. It was a smart retail gimmick of the time, much like a Tupperware home party. The jewelry company held a fashion show at the Embers Restaurant that year, and we fashion show directors felt quite regal parading around showing off our sparkly jewelry while dressed in our favorite finery."

She also recounted a story that she had heard about the Embers: "It's probably one of those urban legends/myths one hears from who knows where, but it seems I vaguely recall the account of some woman dining at the Embers, placing her purse on the floor, missing the mark and unknowingly placing it beyond the line of where the solid floor stopped and the moving floor began. She later found her purse no longer with her when she reached down for it. An alarming upset supposedly ensued until she was calmed by the management, who retrieved her traveling purse, and she was reunited with what we then called her 'pocketbook.'"

For some reason, I don't believe that in this day and time, elegant dining with sweeping vistas would be as appreciated as they were in times past. That is probably why the Embers closed in the early '70s when it fell out of fashion because the "next great thing" was out in the suburbs.

Still, it was comforting to get to go inside the space that once was the Embers. It is now a large meeting room for the Jacksonville Electric Authority, and when I went there to take pictures, the now stationary room was being set up for a retirement party. Although it did not have the "futuristic ambiance" that I had once thought so amazing, it had windows filled with breathtaking views of our lovely Jacksonville, and I couldn't help but be impressed by the beauty of such a great place.

Sadly, when the Embers closed, another piece of our history slipped into antiquity, but to those of us who loved it, we keep it in our memories safely tucked away.

IEYASU OF TOKYO

One downtown restaurant lives vividly in my mind, partly because it had excellent food but mostly because I had never experienced anything like it before.

Ieyasu of Tokyo (or Ieyasu Bistro) was a Japanese restaurant located on Duval Street. It had opened in about 1972, and according to Joe Crea in a July 7, 1983 article in the *Florida Times-Union*, Ieyasu was part of the Takatoshi Yano's chain, which also included two Shogun Restaurants in other parts of Jacksonville.

What I best remember about Ieyasu was that patrons sat on the floor. One would walk in past a small waterfall feature before being shown by kimonoed waitresses to very short tables. There one would take off his or her shoes, as is customary in Japan, step up on a platform and then take a seat on pillows that were on a tatami bamboo mat. For the less adventurous, there were western-style tables and chairs in another part of the restaurant.

Everyone was surrounded by delicious smells from the kitchen and soothing sounds of Japanese flute music from the homeland. Oriental lanterns hung from the ceiling to provide a soft, warm glow of light. Use of chopsticks was encouraged but not mandated, but whether you used a fork or attempted to use chopsticks, you got the sense that you were taking a little trip out of your Jacksonville routine and into the Far East.

The food was excellent and sensibly priced. Teriyaki, tempura and sukiyaki were recommended for the lunch crowd, and shrimp and seafood combinations were best served at dinnertime, when there was a more relaxed atmosphere and the diners didn't have to hurry back to jobs.

Patsy Butterbrodt, a retired educator who now lives in New Tazewell, Tennessee, recalled the exotic nature of Ieyasu's. She and her family went several times when she was a little girl. "You had to leave your shoes off to enter, you sat on large cushions on the floor, and I remember being shocked when I saw all these men in business suits walking around in their stocking feet—tan socks, gray socks, blue socks. I was most impressed." She added, "It was totally Japanese food served by Japanese people. Daddy only took us there for *very* special occasions—I may have gone three times total. But it was right downtown where all the business buildings were. I remember having to cross the river to get there and parking on the downtown street. It was a pretty great place to my father and to me."

In writing this chapter, however, I was once again amazed at how wonderful and flawed memory is. Patsy was certain that she had eaten at Ieyasu of Tokyo in the late '60s. However, when I consulted the Jacksonville business directories for the years 1969 through 1974, there was no mention of Ieyasu of Tokyo. It wasn't until 1975 that it was mentioned as a residence, and it was 1976 that it was listed as a business.

"Wow, that's bizarre. I must have had such a naïve mind to be impressed by socks as a teenager!" Patsy replied when I told her the information I had found. "Hmmmm...I tried looking them up online—seems they relocated to Middleburg, and the original owners now have a little Japanese place there. Again, bizarre!"

A mystery surrounds the present condition of Ieyasu's. I was able to find several articles about Ieyasu of Tokyo, but after 2005, I could find no more.

The *Times-Union* mentioned an attempt by Bill Yano to reopen Ieyasu. On April 21, 1997, an article noted, "The owners of Ieyasu temporarily have closed the downtown Japanese restaurant to concentrate on a new restaurant they opened in Neptune Beach. Bill Yano, whose family owns Ieyasu, said there is no firm timetable for when the Duval Street restaurant will reopen or for a planned remodeling project."

Then, on December 17, 2004, the *Times-Union* ran a review for Ieyasu, saying, "After a devastating fire closed the original restaurant eight years ago, Ieyasu of Tokyo has returned to a new location, and is a welcomed addition to the renaissance of downtown Jacksonville. The new Ieyasu (pronounced E-ya-sue) opened earlier this fall under the culinary leadership of Chef Bobby Humphries, the son of Takatoshi Yano, the founder of the original restaurant."

On October 21, 2005, Dan MacDonald, the food reviewer of the *Florida Times-Union*, said, "No sooner did I pronounce Ieyasu of Tokyo closed in this space last week than it was open again Monday. Here's the story. Owner Robert Humphries has taken ill and the business was closed for two weeks. Brother Bill Humphries, the owner of Shogun Steak and Seafood, 8106 Blanding Blvd., brought over some of his crew Monday to open Ieyasu, 113 W. Adams St., for lunch for the time being. Lunch is served from 11:30 a.m. to 2 p.m. Monday through Friday. A new menu will be posted on the front window each day."

After that, I couldn't find any more information about Ieyasu of Tokyo. Its latest number listed on Internet sites reaches a disconnected phone.

So, I thought I'd try finding Mr. Takatoshi Yano by looking his number up in an old phonebook I had. When I found the only "Yano" in the book, I felt bold and dialed the number. The person who answered sounded as if he were an older gentleman with a heavy Japanese accent.

This person identified himself as Takatoshi Yano, and when I asked if Ieyasu was open, he was emphatic that it was not. He told me Ieyasu had closed in 1988 or the early '90s maybe. He also became obviously pleased when I told him that Ieyasu's had been one of my favorite restaurants. "Thank you. Thank you. Thank you," he said, but I think I should be the one who is grateful for having had the pleasure of ever dining in his wonderful restaurant. It is just sad to say that we are safe in concluding that Ieyasu's is no longer with us, except in memory.

THE GREEN DERBY

One of the nicest stories I heard as I was doing my research on restaurants came from Buddy Ross, a Jacksonville native and retired city employee in the tax collector's office. Sometime not too long after World War II, Buddy and his wife would, on most Saturday nights, join six or seven other couples from their church, the Woodlawn Baptist Church located at Stockton and Roselle Street, and go to the Green Derby in Riverside. The men would wear coats and ties, and the women would wear long, stylish dresses. It was a great deal of fun getting all dolled up to go out. It also didn't hurt that they could feast on steak for $3.95.

The Green Derby was located at the corner of Riverside Avenue and Roselle Street, and according to an article in the *Florida Times-Union* on June 6, 1999, "The Green Derby was a Riverside fixture, hallowed ground for the Sporting Crowd, when the sporting crowd likewise dressed in a classy manner. Start with baked oysters. Greek salad. Filet mignon. Baked potato. A White Cargo. Strawberries in pure cream, served in a champagne glass. A civilization apart from chicken wings in a sports bar."

Sam Kouvaris, sports director at WJXT, Channel 4, met with me for coffee one afternoon to talk about the Green Derby and its impact on sports:

> *People used to reference the Green Derby all the time when I first got to Jacksonville in 1981. Dick Stratton, the sports director at the time at WJXT, was my mentor. He took me under his wing, and he used to tell me many stories about what went on at the Green Derby. Dick would say, "If what went into my eyes and into my ears were to come out of my mouth, then there would be a lot more divorces and firings."*
>
> *Dick may have been prone to hyperbole, and I cannot say for certain if the stories he told me were factual or not, but if you had any connection to sports or were a big star athlete, the Green Derby was where you'd be. Every sports star passing through the South or through north Florida was certain to stop by the Green Derby.*
>
> *It was like the original sports bar, only you didn't need a big-screen TV to see a big star.*

Van Fletcher, the original owner of the Green Derby who died at the age of eighty-three, was "known for his ardent support of sports, charities, and the University of Florida," according to his obituary, written by Jesse-Lynn Kerr in the *Florida Times-Union* on February 22, 1989. Kerr said that Van

Fletcher had opened the Green Derby at the end of World War II, and "before he sold it, the Derby was the preeminent restaurant and lounge. It was known as a sportsman's paradise, and autographed photos of sports heroes lined the walls."

The obituary noted that even though he had never made it out of the sixth grade, Van Fletcher was made an honorary member of the Florida Alumni Association in 1969. After he sold the Green Derby, he continued in the restaurant business with the Derby House restaurants until 1980, and he had, at one time, owned the Towne Pump in San Marco and the Five Points Lounge.

When Fred Abood bought the Green Derby, he continued to provide the excellence that patrons had come to expect. He, too, was a force of nature, if I read things correctly in the final edition of the *Jacksonville Journal* on October 28, 1988. It reported that Abood was a Jacksonville native, "a product of parochial school, a Navy veteran, a former salesman at Simon's Cash Store on West Ninth Street, across from Beulah Beal [Elementary School]."

He began his restaurant career in the kitchen of Joe Adeeb's Steer Room and bought it four years later. From 1952 to 1972, he became the Steer Room's "genial host. His customers were his friends. Thursday's luncheon was Arabic food. He would buy you a drink."

He then bought the Green Derby, and it became one of a very few restaurants that aged its beef. Its menu offered quite a variety of gourmet dishes: lamb, Long Island duckling in orange sauce, baked kibbee and breast of capon in wild rice. And still it maintained its reputation as a place to go to enjoy sports, especially after Gator Bowl and college games.

One thing that made the Green Derby such a great place was the excellent cooking. According to the *Florida Times-Union* on September 8, 1968, Fred Abood's Green Derby received a letter from the prestigious Union International D'Organizations Nationales D'Hotleiers, Restauranteurs, et Cafetiers (Ho-Re-Ca) in early July 1968. The letter noted that the Green Derby was "exemplifying the highest degree of excellence and thus being eligible to stand among those already affiliated with this organization…It is with the greatest pleasure that I wish to inform you that the Selection Committee of the International Ho-Re-Ca has advised me that it has tentatively agreed to the recognition of Fred Abood's Green Derby Restaurant." By August 1968, the Green Derby's inclusion into the Internationale Ho-Re-Ca was confirmed.

The decline of the Green Derby probably began when Abood retired in 1982. He sold the restaurant to three investors, but by 1985, the restaurant had closed. In 1986, Blue Cross and Blue Shield bought the property and razed the building with the distinctive mustachioed logo and derby hat to make way for a parking lot. Fred Abood died on May 24, 1999.

Whether one went to the Green Derby for the excellent food, for the opportunity to dress up or for the game day gatherings and celebrations, it was a fantastic, fancy place where people really wanted to go to enjoy the best life has to offer. Van Fletcher and Fred Abood both saw to it that the Green Derby was one of the best spots in the city.

HOTEL RESTAURANTS

There once was a time in Jacksonville history when "a night on the town" meant a fine meal and dancing afterward. Imagine how magical it must have been to enjoy live music—the old standards and the big band sound— as you dined on the finest of dishes prepared by great chefs and served by capable waiters.

During that golden time, Jacksonville could boast of many such wonderful places, especially at the downtown hotels—the George Washington Hotel, the Mayflower Hotel, the Robert Meyer Hotel and the Roosevelt Hotel. (Jacksonville hotels were often named with the word "Hotel" in front of the name, as in "Hotel George Washington." However, everyday local usage usually places the word "Hotel" after the name.) Each provided wonderful nighttime dinner and dancing experiences for the people of Jacksonville. In their heyday, these hotels not only provided great entertainment, but they also were wonderful places for conventions, weddings, bar mitzvahs and bat mitzvahs, birthdays and anniversaries.

The Mayflower Hotel had its "Finest Roof Garden in the South," something that was only slightly visible on the postcard. The Robert Meyer Hotel, a place where my high school's prom breakfast was served, could also brag of the Bali H'ai and the Café Carib. In an article in the *Florida Times-Union* on May 13, 1956, it was reported that the Robert Meyer was opened in 1959 and was named for a pilot who flew with the Flying Tiger Squadron in World War II. That pilot was the father of Owner John E. Meyer.

But there were two other hotel entertainment venues that really stood out: the George Washington Hotel and the Roosevelt Hotel. The George

Above: Mayflower Hotel. *Courtesy of the Florida State Photographic Archives.*

Opposite, top: Robert Meyer Hotel. *Courtesy of the Florida State Photographic Archives.*

Opposite, bottom: Postcard of the "Rainbow Room" in the George Washington Hotel. *Courtesy of the Jacksonville Public Library's Florida Collection.*

George Ludwig Orchestra performing in the Rainbow Room of the George Washington Hotel. *Courtesy of Ivy Ludwig Eyrick.*

Washington Hotel, according to a January 22, 1974 article in the *Times-Union*, was built in 1926 and was touted as being the first completely air-conditioned hotel in the United States. It was torn down in 1974.

The Rainbow Room was the biggest dining place for the George Washington Hotel, and it lives on fondly in the memories of many Jacksonville residents. Etta Fialkow, a retired teacher, said, "The Rainbow Room, probably after the famous Rainbow Room in New York City, had a live band, and my parents took me there for my birthday when I was young. The band played and sang 'Happy Birthday' to me. I thought I was hot stuff!"

Jacksonville resident Ivy Ludwig Eyrick knows a lot about that band. For twenty years, her father—a drummer who had played with Kay Keiser's band—was the head of the group George Ludwig and His Orchestra.

George Ludwig was originally from Philadelphia, and during World War II, he served in the Fifth Infantry and played in the U.S. Army Band. After the war, he went to Miami and played in many of the clubs there before coming to play at the Peacock Club on Philips Highway in Jacksonville. The Peacock Club was a "happening" place in its time during the '40s. It was a casino of sorts, and it was here that George met his wife, Bebe Parnell, originally from South Carolina, who was the hatcheck girl there. After a three-month courtship, they were married.

Ivy told me of some memories:

> *My father's band consisted of a piano and drums, trumpet, sax and clarinet, and for my eighth birthday, I got to celebrate up in the balcony, as we did back in those days. Of course, most of the time, people just came there for dinner and dancing.*
>
> *There were some other special times for me. They had these things called marathons to raise money for charities, and famous people would come to help—Roy Rogers was one and Chester, Doc and Miss Kitty from the television show* Gunsmoke *were some others. I loved it because I got to get everyone's autograph. I also remember one time when Chester* [Dennis Weaver] *jumped over a row of chairs. Not exactly sure why, but they made a big deal about it.* [It is possible that this stunt was a "big deal" because the character Weaver played on Gunsmoke had been wounded in the Civil War and walked with a stiff-legged gait.]
>
> *Every night, my father started the show by saying, "Good evening ladies and gentleman, and welcome to the beautiful Rainbow Room. Now with the playing of our theme song 'Ivy,' this is yours truly, George Ludwig and the Orchestra, inviting you all to dance."*

It was no accident that Ivy was named for that theme song.

Another hotel with an elegant venue for dinner and dancing experiences was the Roosevelt Hotel. Its Patio Lounge was a "happening place" as far back as the '30s, and as the postcards attest, the place was often packed. It holds a humorous place in the heart of Jacksonville native Kathy O'Leary Gallun, who e-mailed me this story:

> *One time my folks gave me permission to take a date to the Roosevelt Club private restaurant at the Roosevelt Hotel. Ed Hartley from Bishop Kenny was my date. He was captain of the football team at the time and a really nice guy. We were alone at dinner and trying to be grown-up. Everything happened like an episode from* I Love Lucy. *My step-dad, Jim Aldous, had told the matre'd that we could each have one cocktail with our dinner.*

Newspaper advertisement for the Rainbow Room of the George Washington Hotel. *Courtesy of Ivy Ludwig Eyrick.*

Patio Room of Roosevelt Hotel. *Courtesy of the Florida State Photographic Archives.*

Poor Ed was so stressed that he missed his mouth with his glass of water. I thought I would give him a few minutes to compose himself, so I excused myself from the table and headed to the ladies room. I did not realize that I had tucked the table cloth into my waistband along with my napkin. When I got up and started walking, the entire table cloth came with me. We both started grabbing table items to prevent them from crashing to the floor. The waiter came over and helped us unload our booty back to the table.

I chose cognac as my cocktail since I had seen it in the movies. We toasted and I felt the drink eroding my throat away. I coughed, sputtered, turned red and sweaty, all while trying to act sophisticated. The sophisticated part did not work. On our way home we were in a fender bender with five cars. Poor Ed was driving the last car. We decided it was not worth the risk to try another date. Ed Hartley was a swell guy, but the fickle finger of fate squished us.

Elaine Pennywitt Danese, a native of Jacksonville, remembered the Roosevelt Hotel from when she was a very little girl. "I remember having Shirley Temples and dancing on the top of my daddy's shoes. Oh yeah, and I remember that a woman went from table to table with a tray, selling packs of cigarettes to the customers. Certainly a different time."

John Thomas, a well-known television newscaster for Jacksonville's WJXT, Channel 4, shared coffee with me on a wonderful Jacksonville Beach morning, talking about his many talents and many connections to so many restaurants and hotels of long ago. As we talked for about two hours, it seemed to me that he had probably performed, singing and playing piano, at most of the venues where live music was celebrated—country clubs, restaurants, retirement communities, lounges and hotels.

Thomas grew up in Wilmington, North Carolina, and got his start in broadcasting when he was about seventeen when he became a disc jockey for a little radio station housed above a Sherwin-Williams paint store. He was in the navy in 1960, assigned to the USS *Saratoga*, when he first came to Jacksonville. He got to play at the opening of the officers' club at Mayport, and this was his introduction into Jacksonville's music community. He met many local musicians with whom he would later play.

When he got out of the navy, he returned to Jacksonville and went into television. He and Bill Grove were the six o'clock news anchors for Channel 4 until Thomas moved to the eleven o'clock news time slot years later. In his free time, though, he would join with or form bands that would play all over this area.

A self-taught piano player, John Thomas still performs locally, and he can provide any venue with "a Single to Trio to Full Band," but what I was most interested in finding out was what it was like to play in a venue like the Roosevelt Hotel.

"There was an upstairs hideaway for the politicians called the Spa. They could play poker up there, smoke cigars and just get away from it all, you know. But I played in the Roosevelt's dining room the same night that the Roosevelt fire broke out and claimed so many lives. Of course, there was absolutely no indication that a fire was going to happen when I was performing. Nothing. I had finished my gig and gone home for the night. Then, early in the morning, the station [Channel 4] called, and I had to run back to the station to cover the breaking news about the tragedy. As a matter of fact, my one and only byline in the *Washington Post*, which owned Channel 4, was about that fire."

The Roosevelt Hotel had many elegant rooms in which to dine and dance, and it was indeed a most elegant place for going out and celebrating, but for many in Jacksonville, the Roosevelt is most remembered for the fire that took the lives of twenty-one people on December 29, 1963.

The *Florida Times-Union* ran a story on December 30 with a lead paragraph that read, "Fire in a second story ballroom just off the main lobby gushed smoke and gasses through the packed Roosevelt Hotel yesterday morning, resulting in 21 deaths and injuries to 65 others." The article went on to report that most of the deaths were from asphyxiation. The other deaths came when a woman fell to her death from an upper story and when an assistant fire chief died of a heart attack while engaged in rescue efforts. One of the rescued survivors was Donna Axum, 1964's Miss America.

Thomas remembered that the Gator Bowl had filled the city with many tourists that weekend who had attended the game. "Dick Stratton [another famous on-air Channel 4 personality] had reserved a room at the Roosevelt, and when the station was unable to contact him after the news broke, there was great concern that he might have been caught up in the fire. Thankfully, Dick had gone to the beach with his friends and decided to stay there for the night."

After that event, the Roosevelt Hotel was never the same. The hotel was closed in 1964 and eventually became a retirement home until 1989. It was placed on the National Register of Historic Places in 1991. Presently, it is an upscale apartment building called the Carling on West Adams Street.

PART II
Over the River

THE LOBSTER HOUSE RESTAURANT AND THE DOLPHIN RESTAURANT, MARINELAND, FLORIDA

Many of us of a certain age can remember going to some pretty awful B-movies in theaters around town either with dates or in groups of friends. It didn't matter because we jumped at the chance to get away from home and homework.

Most natives of Jacksonville are aware that in the early days of cinema, our fair city and the north Florida area were the settings of many movies before Hollywood lured the industry to California. One production company, however, came here in 1954 to make the sequel of *Creature from the Black Lagoon*, a B-movie extraordinaire that was corny and scientifically questionable. A "gillman" from a body of water in the Amazon jungles terrorizes a group of scientists on an expedition.

The sequel, the B-movie classic *Revenge of the Creature* (1955), starred John Agar, Lori Nelson and John Bromfield. It picks up the story with different scientists going back to the Amazon and bringing the "gillman" back to the United States for further study. They capture him and then put him in a place that looks suspiciously like Marineland (which is where they filmed many scenes). Amazingly, the creature escapes and then terrorizes

Jacksonville, most specifically the patrons of the Lobster House, an iconic restaurant of an earlier Jacksonville.

Elizabeth Basille, a longtime employee of USF&G Insurance Company and native of Jacksonville, was in her early twenties when she and her friends witnessed with their own eyes the attack of the monster. She really relishes being part of this historic event.

"We had heard that the film crew was going to be there [at the Lobster House], but we were young and we just walked right back where they were filming, and no one stopped us. Still, it really was scary even though we knew it was just a movie they were making. Seeing this creature crawling up and out of the water—I'll never forget it!"

The Lobster House Restaurant on the south side of the St. Johns River was more than just a movie setting, however. It was a very popular seafood restaurant that also served steak and other non-seafood dishes. There are even pictures of Fuller Warren, the thirtieth governor of Florida and the man for whom our bridge is named, enjoying himself there.

The Lobster House was built in 1944 on a dock at the foot of the St. Elmo Acosta Bridge, with the Main Street Bridge on its other side. The restaurant was owned and operated by Irving D. "Ducky" Glickstein, and there were water taxis available between the restaurant and the courthouse and city hall. Tourists loved the place, as did sports fans. Often there was live entertainment—beyond that of monsters crawling out of the St. Johns River.

Sadly, on Monday, December 17, 1962, the Lobster House, which operated in a fifty-seven-year-old wooden structure, burned down. The headline in the December 1962 *Florida Times-Union* read, "Restaurant Fire Loss Is $63,000." The article, written by Charles Cook, noted, "The fire was first discovered at 1:25 a.m. by Police Sergeant H.W. Keeler and Patrolman H. Haskins, who turned in the alarm…A cigarette apparently started the blaze. Damage was extensive because the building's fire sprinkler system had burst during last week's extreme cold and servicemen had not been able to repair it earlier."

Later, in the article, Glickstein is quoted as saying, "It [the Lobster House] was an old, wooden-framed structure, and I seriously doubt if the city would allow me to replace it as such under the latest building codes…The Lobster House will have to be rebuilt with masonry, but the concrete slab now wouldn't support masonry. We'll probably have to move to higher ground and start from the bottom up." Thankfully, Glickstein was fully insured, but he did not rebuild the Lobster House.

Lobster House Aerial View. *Author postcard.*

Lobster House interior. *Author postcard.*

Dolphin Restaurant and Lounge. *Author postcard.*

The *Jacksonville Journal* of October 28, 1988, reported that Jerome and Paul Fletcher built a new building on the site of the old Lobster House in the late '60s. It was the "sizzling Some Place Else" discotheque, but that is a whole different story.

I do think it is important to mention an interesting connection between the Lobster House and another famous restaurant *not* in Jacksonville. In Marineland, Florida, near St. Augustine, there is another lost restaurant close to another setting for the movie *Return of the Creature.*

Marineland was the first of its kind—a wonderful oceanarium where trained dolphins put on shows for the tourists, and tanks were filled with sea life and had portholes where tourists could enjoy seascapes. It was in these tanks that most of the underwater scenes of the movie were filmed. It is also the place from which the gillman escapes before he makes his way to Jacksonville, where he will terrorize the good people living there. The Dolphin Restaurant and Lounge was part of the Marineland complex, and it was at the Dolphin that a very famous meeting took place. It was here where Ernest Hemingway and Marjorie Kinnan Rawlings met and dined together.

Rodger L. Tarr wrote an excellent article in the *Hemingway Review*, and in it he tells a story I had heard before, probably in one of my literature classes long ago. Tarr said, "As the story goes, Rawlings noticed Hemingway and Martha Gellhorn, later his third wife, at a table across the room. Rawlings sent him a note: 'Are you Ernest Hemingway?' Hemingway responded: 'If you are Marjorie Rawlings, I am.'"

In researching the Dolphin Restaurant, I really wanted to be sure that this story was true before I included it in my book. I consulted a book of letters called *Max and Marjorie*—the correspondence between the editor Max Perkins and Rawlings. According to a letter written by Rawlings and dated September 19, 1940, "We had an unexpected and very jolly meeting with Ernest Hemingway and Martha Gellhorn. I was entertaining over the weekend for Julia and our party was at Marineland at dinner. I recognized Hemingway at a nearby table and spoke to him. They joined us for drinks and then came up to the cottage and stayed much later than was wise for them."

Perhaps the note part of this legendary meeting is hard to verify, since even scholars cite the source by saying "as the story goes…," but I like to think that it is true. All we can know for certain is that Ernest and Marjorie did share a meal at the Dolphin Restaurant. And how wonderful it would have been to be there! I can just imagine the ultra-masculine Ernest tossing back his whiskey while laughing at some amusing anecdote Marjorie had just shared about life in the wilds of north Florida. But since I have watched and rewatched the movie, *Revenge of the Creature*, my fantasy now includes an uninvited glimpse of an escaped "gillman," walking like a zombie on his way to the Lobster House, terrorizing the patrons as he stumbles past the ocean-view picture window of the restaurant. So much for a lively imagination.

SOME PLACE ELSE, DIAMOND HEAD, HARBORMASTER, CRAWDADDY'S AND SURFSIDE 6

The Southbank of the St. Johns River has supported many restaurants; but the area was and is not necessarily conducive to restaurant longevity. Many of the places I researched were like bottle rockets—dazzling displays of splendor that ran their courses and then fizzled out with pitiful whimpers.

Once the Lobster House burned down, the owners decided not to rebuild over the water because a replacement building would need to meet newer codes. A new building could not be supported by the dock that remained

Matchbooks for Some Place Else, Harbormasters (locally just called Harbormaster), Diamond Head and Crawdaddy's Restaurants. *Courtesy of Barbara Lewis Milano and Claire Fleming King.*

after the fire, so any restaurant would have to be built on the land. After ownership of the property passed from Glickstein to Jerome and Paul Fletcher, the brothers built Some Place Else on the property adjacent to where the old Lobster House once was.

Claire Fleming King, a retired phone company employee, remembered going to Some Place Else rather regularly on Fridays and Saturday nights:

This was one of my favorite places to go between 1970 and 1977. It was the hippest, friendliest and safest place to go. It was downtown without being "downtown." The patrons were well-dressed, well-mannered and up-and-coming men and women. They were there "networking" before it was called "networking."

Sometimes, celebrities who were starring at an Alhambra Dinner Theatre Production dined there. Local notables often stopped by the bar after a late stay at the office. There was a huge bar by the front entrance with a lower-level dance floor with small tables on the other side of the room. I remember the sounds of Carol King, the Bee Gees and Three Dog Night blasting from the speakers. The dining room overlooked the river and a beautiful view of the north bank and the lights of downtown Jacksonville. The restaurant with both tables and booths had a décor that was pure '70s, with mod posters on the wall and paintings in each booth.

When ownership of Some Place Else changed hands, the name was changed to Diamond Head Lobster House, and it became a going concern for about eight or nine years. It specialized in great Polynesian food and sponsored a lobster race on the night before the Florida/Georgia football game. Then progress took its toll, and the St. Elmo Acosta Bridge was to be replaced and widened.

An April 15, 1986 article by Ford Risley, business writer for the *Florida Times-Union*, noted, "Diamond Head Lobster House and Crab Trappers was closed last week to get ready for the opening of Harbormaster, a new restaurant being built on the river next to Diamond Head." Later in the article, he wrote, "State officials had told [Fred] Levy and co-owner Pat Wachholz that Diamond Head would eventually have to be demolished to make room for a new span to replace the Acosta Bridge…'We're in transition from moving there to here,' Levy said yesterday at the Harbormaster construction site. He would not give specific date of the closing. Harbormaster is scheduled to open this summer, he said."

Harbormaster, which once operated in the place now called River City Brewing Company, suffered a whole host of problems almost from the beginning. In a January 20, 2013 column by Ron Littlepage for the *Florida Times-Union*, he delineated the sequence of events:

Things went well for a while [with Harbormaster], *but then came a year's long sad saga of lawsuits, changes in ownership, foreclosure, default on a federal loan backed by the city, more lawsuits and unpaid rent.*

Harbormaster Restaurant. *Courtesy of the Florida State Photographic Archives.*

Crawdaddy's Restaurant. *Courtesy of the Florida State Photographic Archives.*

After the city ended up owning the building—it already owned the land—Harbormaster became a running joke about City Hall's ineptitude.

Harbormasters Restaurant, which failed last year despite a $2.9 million taxpayer-backed loan, is still providing some of the best eating in Jacksonville.

Finally, in 1993, River City Brewing bought out the previous owners, and it has been operating a 325-seat restaurant and microbrewery in its beautiful location ever since.

Another ill-fated restaurant by the river was the "eccentric" Crawdaddy's. It was located a bit farther down the St. Johns, right next to the Duval County School Board Building on Prudential Drive, and it was a radical concept that didn't always sit well with everyone.

Crawdaddy's Restaurant was a concept restaurant that was, at the very least, interesting. In an April 2, 1983 article in the *Times-Union* written by staff writer Denise Smith, it was reported that Crawdaddy's was developed by a company called Specialty Restaurants. David C. Tallichet Jr. was the junior vice-president of the company and had used twenty themes in the company's fifty restaurants nationwide. Crawdaddy's was the "1930s fish-camp motif," which was "one of the more popular of the themes."

As the article noted, "Crawdaddy's exterior is covered with rusty tin and burnt, craggy wood. Two fishing boats, which look like they will never sail again, augment the scraggy appearance of the front yard. Uneven wood beams and rusted steel bolts and brackets give the building the look of a shack." Apparently, not everyone was as happy with the design as was Specialty Restaurants Inc. The article added, "Criticism of the restaurant's appearance has bothered Tallichet—whose business is to entertain, not offend…In response to the criticism, the company planted small trees in front of Crawdaddy's in hopes of softening the appearance of the raw exterior, he said…'I would hope that after our landscaping had become more mature, there will be less offence.'"

As I recall, the food was in the Cajun tradition, and I found it too hot for my taste, but the interior was actually quite elegant. There were antiques and period pieces throughout. There was even a moose head mounted over the bar that had been in the movie *The Four Seasons*.

On March 29, 2002, an article announced in the *Florida Times-Union* that Crawdaddy's was closed for remodeling, but two years later, an article on June 15, 2004, reported that Crawdaddy's was to be demolished. It is presently just a field.

Finally, before I leave the Southbank, I need to mention an interesting "almost" restaurant. There was an attempt to bring Surfside 6 to the Diamond Head waterfront to possibly serve as a restaurant while construction and demolishing was taking place during the widening of the Acosta Bridge.

An article ran in the April 12, 1983 *Florida Times-Union*, announcing the arrival of Surfside 6, a houseboat that had served as the setting of an ABC detective television show (1960–62). The storyline was that Troy Donahue, Van Williams and Lee Patterson solved crimes while living on a houseboat at Surfside 6 in Miami Beach. The article noted that the very boat used in the TV series was a "two level boat, which will be used as a restaurant next to Diamond Head."

While all of this sounds great, I can find no article anywhere that says this place ever even opened. I did find a July 30, 1983 article in the *Times-Union* by Phillip Fiorini with a headline that read, "Dr. Hopes TV's Surfside 6 Boat Floats in Plans for Riverwalk Restaurant Venture."

Dr. Lewis J. Obi had bought the boat, being somewhat sentimental about it since he drove past it every day when he was in medical school in Miami, the article had said. Then, it detailed all his hopes for the houseboat and the problems he continued to have that prevented him from getting the restaurant up and running.

After that article, I checked the Jacksonville business directories for 1983, 1984, 1985 and 1986 and could find no listing for Surfside 6 for the period during which it would have been open. The only other mention of the Surfside 6 houseboat was in an article that ran in the *Chicago Tribune* in 1997 that noted that the builder of Surfside 6 thought that the boat was a restaurant in Jacksonville.

No one I asked had ever heard of Surfside 6 as a restaurant. Some remembered the TV show, but beyond that, nothing. Still, it would have been so cool!

BISER'S RESTAURANTS

There once was a restaurant logo that became synonymous with great seafood. A huge red snapper sign trimmed in red neon hung over one of Jacksonville's most iconic restaurants. In a November 6, 1966 article written by Sherrel Rhoades in the *Florida Times-Union*, it was reported that Howard

Downtown Biser's Restaurant. *Courtesy of the Florida State Photographic Archives.*

Biser came to Jacksonville just after the turn of the century with little more than pocket change. He waited tables at the old Gilreath and Sharkey Eatery located on Bay Street, where he began to learn the restaurant business.

When he was still in his twenties, he formed a partnership that created Bingham & Biser's Restaurant on Forsyth Street. They later moved to 211 Forsyth, where the restaurant slowly consumed almost an entire block. It was at this location that Biser made his famous red snapper the specialty of the house. It was only natural that he would use as a logo a big red fish.

In the late '30s, Biser moved the restaurant to 207 West Duval. Even in 1966, the big red snapper sign still hung at that address, though Biser's had been gone for years.

Biser's opened at King Street on the Southside, where it remained until 1959. Then it moved to the Arlington Expressway to provide a restaurant for the Holiday Inn. From there, it went to the Heart of Jacksonville Motor Lodge in 1965. In 1968, it closed its doors for good.

The article continued, saying that Biser's enjoyed a wonderful reputation. It was even one of the charter members on that select list "recommended by Duncan Hines Club." Biser's Restaurant stayed on that list until the club dissolved. Even so, when the club disbanded, Biser's was one of fewer than a dozen restaurants from the eastern seaboard left on the list.

Biser's Restaurant at Philips Highway Location. *Courtesy of the Florida State Photographic Archives.*

David Seitz, nephew of Howard Biser, spoke very fondly of his uncle. "My uncle knew everybody's name, and he worked back in the time when it was important to have the freshest seafood. He went to the docks to get it himself. And he was proud of his kitchen. People would actually enter the restaurant that way. My father inherited the restaurant when my uncle died in the early '50s, and I have worked in the restaurant business myself since I sold out in 2006, when I was operating twenty barbeque restaurants in St. Louis."

For Buddy Ross, a retired finance and budget control supervisor at the tax collector's office, Biser's was a special time that he got to spend with his grandparents. When he was newly married right after World War II, his grandparents would invite him and his new bride to dinner at Biser's Restaurant. Buddy and his wife would have to catch a bus from their apartment to the corner of Eighteenth and Laura, where his grandmother and grandfather lived. From there, they would take his grandfather's Buick over the bridge and out to Biser's on Kings Avenue (soon to become Philips Highway). There was only one rule: they were to eat whatever they wanted.

Charlie Robertson, the songwriter from St. Augustine, shared a memory he had of going to Biser's. "My girlfriend's mother took us to Biser's, and I disgraced myself when mints were served after the meal. They were served with a spoon, and I took a spoonful and put it right in my mouth, not realizing the mints were to be placed on the plate and passed on to everybody else. I can just see my date's mother rolling her eyes at my faux pas."

Another story I heard came from D.H. Eaton, local author. "My brother went to work for Biser's Restaurant as a busboy. He usually went there after school or on weekends, and it was an all-you-can-eat kind of place. Employees could eat what they wanted. It wasn't long before they let him go. When he asked why, they informed him, 'Well, frankly you eat too much.'"

Nancy Blackmer, who still resides in Jacksonville, had a sweet memory about Biser's. "I went to the prom with Howard Seitz. Howard was adopted by the Biser family. So, when we went out to dinner the night of the prom, in all our full formal attire, we naturally went to Biser's out on Main Street. It was not a 'formal' type restaurant, and I remember feeling very out of place in my pink, floor length dress."

Ivy Eyrick, whose father was a local band leader at the George Washington, also remembered Biser's. "On Sundays after church, my father would park in the back of Biser's, and we would walk right through the kitchen to get to our table. Funny how you remember odd things like that."

The big red fish logo may be long gone, but thoughts of delicious, fresh seafood are never lost in the recollections of Jacksonville's Biser's patrons. Perhaps they are the yardstick by which all other fish dinners are measured.

STRICKLAND'S FAMILY RESTAURANTS

Strickland's Seafood in Mayport was the first of the franchise of five restaurants. It was located near the Mayport Ferry landing for a very long time. When I sat down to lunch with Michael Strickland at Al's Pizza in Atlantic Beach, he had many stories of life as a restaurant worker and owner:

> *Way back in my grandfather's day, before there was a base at Mayport, the navy wanted a place that could at least serve breakfast to the workers who would be building it. So, he and his brother opened a restaurant to do just that. Eventually, they started serving lunch there as well. At the beginning, there were four or five stools and several tables and booths. Locals started coming, and business was amazing.*
>
> *In the early '50s, the state needed a place to put a ferry, so a deal was struck. My family would "loan" the state the property to build a ferry launch so long as the property came back to the family if the ferries ever shut down. And our restaurant was right there next to all the traffic. At one time, there were four ferries running, like before I-95 was built. During those days, people would line up for two blocks waiting to get in the restaurant."*

Strickland's Seafood at Mayport. *Courtesy of the Jacksonville Public Library's Florida Collection.*

Strickland's postcard. *Courtesy of the Jacksonville Public Library's Florida Collection.*

According to the *Jacksonville Journal's* last edition in 1988, the original Strickland's (that also had a general store) was opened in 1935 by B.J. "Uncle Ben" Strickland and was called Strickland & Sons. In 1945, the sons, Benjamin "B.J." Strickland and W.F. Strickland, took the restaurant over and renamed it Strickland Brothers Restaurant. In 1971, B.J. acquired the business, and three years later in 1974, a fire destroyed the building. A new five-hundred-seat restaurant reopened in 1977, and Mayport residents and shrimpers were all invited to an opening party.

The article noted that Strickland's Seafood could brag of a lounge, an oyster bar, a fish market and five dining areas. For a very short time, it had a floating addition called Riverboat Sally, which sank at dawn about two months after opening. As the restaurant grew older, it began to become a bit more upscale, with a very fine reputation for its great seafood: fresh fish, baked oysters and smoked mullet dip. But in 1985, the restaurant was sold at a foreclosure sale and reopened by D.G. Granger. In 1988, it was owned by John Podamsky.

The next Strickland's Seafood Michael told me about was at Jacksonville Beach. "My father and uncle were partners, and when the old Wagon Wheel became available on North First Street, Jacksonville Beach, my father left the Mayport restaurant to open the other Strickland's at the beach."

One of the best stories Michael Strickland shared was about the night the Rolling Stones came and had a late supper at the Jacksonville Beach location where he was managing.

> *I get a call on a Saturday night as we were preparing to close. The guy said he was the general manager of the Rolling Stones, like I would know what that meant. They wanted us to keep the place open past hours so the band could come and eat after their concert. I said okay, and when I told the cook, he became really excited. "I'll be glad to cook for them!" At about 10:45, the Stones drive up in a black limousine and sneak in the back way so they don't attract anyone's attention. Mick Jagger was very nice. They were all very nice and polite, and they tipped the waitress $100. Their visit was even mentioned in an article in* Rolling Stone *magazine.*

Strickland's Town House was the third location of the Strickland's franchise, and it was another fabled restaurant located at 3510 Philips Highway. It was especially important to many other businesses.

Duke Mitchell, a retired underwriter for the USF&G Insurance Company, remembered well many business-related gatherings at Strickland's Town

House. He said, "This was a place USF&G used to take officers who came in from Baltimore, which was the home office of the company. And we often entertained insurance agents here as well. It was a really nice place. Since I didn't drink, I became the designated driver, so everyone enjoyed the big bar while we were entertained by live bands and music."

In the last *Jacksonville Journal* article of 1988, Joyce Phelps wrote that Strickland's Town House was opened in 1959 by Benjamin "B.J." Strickland and his brother W.F. Strickland. This was a not only a great place for businessmen to entertain clients and bosses, but politicians often ate there as well. There is even mention of a parking lot altercation between Dan Scarborough and John Lanahan that made the news in the late '60s.

There were many other less intense experiences at Strickland's Town House. Sheldon Fages, legal administrator at the Hyatt & Stubblefield, PC, law firm and who currently lives in Duluth, Georgia, said, "About forty-three years ago, Sherry Siegel Fages and I had our engagement party at Strickland's Town House on Philips Highway. As Sherry's mom, Jean Siegel, was the manager of 5-7-9 Shops at Regency Square, Sherry always had really neat outfits. At the engagement dinner, she wore this chocolate brown dress with sheer, see-through sleeves. Boy, was she hot! I can't remember what I had for breakfast yesterday, but I sure remember that outfit she wore that night."

Ellen Ruffner Pierce, a Southside resident, has some very tender memories of Strickland's Town House:

> *My family had moved here from New Jersey when my father, who worked for Prudential, was transferred here. We lived on Temple Drive when we first came here, and he would work all week at Prudential. On Friday and Saturday nights, he would play at the Crystal Lounge in Lakewood Shopping Center. There were times when he played with Virginia Atter Keyes and Tommy Woods even.*
>
> *But, on Sunday afternoons, my father would play the organ at the Strickland's Town House, and my family got to eat there for free. We could eat anything we wanted. My mother would order duck, which I found rather greasy. I went for things like spaghetti, but it was always very special.*
>
> *Then, in the middle of the night, probably in 1955 or '56, the phone rang, and we were told that the Town House had burned down. Everyone was very sad.*

I asked Michael Strickland if he remembered a fire at the Town House, and he said that he didn't recall any. "Fires happen all the time

Strickland's Town House interior. *Courtesy of the Jacksonville Public Library's Florida Collection.*

in restaurants, so maybe there was one, but it didn't shut them down or I would have remembered that."

What I do know is that by 1988, when Phelps wrote her final column, Strickland's Town House was vacant and no more. Michael said that there is just a vacant lot where the Mayport Strickland's Seafood once stood. He said that the building was torn down years ago. And the two other Strickland's sites, which were exclusively takeout places, were gone as well.

Michael, however, is still going strong. After he retired from the restaurant and fish business, he began writing novels. His *The Red Cotton Fields* is doing quite well as an eBook on Amazon. Even though all five of the Strickland's Restaurants and takeout places are just memories, I bet they just might become the settings in one of Michael's upcoming novels.

HOWARD JOHNSON'S RESTAURANTS

His name was Howard Deering Johnson, and he was an ice cream–making fool. He came up with twenty-eight flavors, to be exact, as well as an incredible variety of decadent confections that were stored in treasure chest–freezers behind his gleaming counters.

According to his colorful placemats, Howard had a drugstore in Massachusetts where he stocked fresh, homemade ice cream. Eventually, he expanded beyond his twenty-eight flavors of ice cream to include hot dogs and fried clam strip sandwiches, eventually moving on to clean, well-lit restaurants and motels. The roofs of his establishments were orange, and all interior colors were coordinated around a turquoise theme. Carpets, counters, bedspreads, uniforms—somehow, it all blended together with that dazzling combination.

No matter where in America you went, you'd find Howard Johnson's restaurants reassuringly the same, and no matter which Howard Johnson's you chose, the ice cream served there had to be the best made anywhere in the world. I guess that's why Americans flocked to HOJOs everywhere—even to the ones in Jacksonville, Florida, and the ones on Golfair Boulevard and Lane Avenue, where I worked during the summers of 1969, '70 and '72.

I reported dutifully every waitressing day at 5:00 a.m. and rarely left before 3:30 p.m. I dressed in a turquoise, houndstooth A-line shirtwaist dress and huge, white orthopedic shoes, with my long hair in a bun that was tucked into a regulation net. I met with a smile the hordes of tourists heading through Jacksonville on their way south to Daytona or Miami or back north on their way home. It was my pleasure to serve ice cream delights, clam strip sandwiches and three-course meals to these souls from all over the United States and Canada. And I considered myself lucky to collect ten dollars per day in tips, for all those beyond-the-most-basic things I would need at college.

Howard Johnson's was a place that your mother might want to take you. The food was not fancy by any stretch of the imagination, but it was all good for you. Your piping-hot entrée came with rolls and salad. Ice cream was for dessert. The place had a very '50s or '60s feel about it—maybe it was the décor, but I always felt like I was home when I went there.

Others have similar feelings. Dolly Fleet Corlin, a retired educator currently living in Colorado, said, "My parents, Joel and Margaret, enjoyed going there as much as we did. My parents took us there as a special treat after report cards. And I remember their mocha chip ice cream!"

Author D.H. Eaton recalled that "Howard Johnson's was the location of my first 'date,' or to clarify, my second stop on my first 'date.' I was invited by a fellow Englewood Elementary sixth-grade student to accompany him to the patrol boy dance. His father drove us (of course), then picked us up and

Howard Johnson's restaurant at Philips. *Courtesy of the Jacksonville Public Library's Florida Collection.*

drove us on to Howard Johnson's on Philips Highway for ice cream cones. I don't recall the flavor I chose, but I can still bring to memory the lovely wrist corsage the boy gave me."

At the present time, all Howard Johnson's restaurants in our area are gone. The restaurants once numbered more than one thousand locations in the United States at the peak of their popularity, but now only two remain in the entire country. According to the website www.hojoland.com only the Lake Placid, New York Howard Johnson's restaurant and the one in Bangor, Maine, are still open today, and the one at Lake Placid is for sale.

The website noted that a major sale to a foreign concern in the '80s called for the diversification of the company, and this signaled the end of the franchise. I think, however, that this might not have been all of it. More trendy places came along and stole us away from the "comfy, family feel" of our parents' restaurant. I suppose that my connection to this franchise really colors my opinion of the place, but I cannot help but long for the days when going out meant going to Howard Johnson's as a reward for good grades, comforting food when traveling or just a cool, delightful treat consisting of one of the twenty-eight ice cream flavors.

Joann's Chili Bordello

One of the most enduring memories I have of Joann's Chili Bordello was the engagement party for my brother-in-law, David, and his fiancée, Cheryl. When we arrived, we entered a dark, intimate space and were soon ushered into a private area. I was immediately impressed/shocked with the "interesting" dress of the waitresses—something you'd have expected to see in a saloon of the Old West, or worse. These women were dressed in costumes my mother would have considered beyond scandalous.

The waitresses wore low-cut bustiers, and they had frilly garter belts holding up silk stockings. It was all in fun, of course—in keeping with the name of the business, after all. The best part, however, came when one of our party, Bob, said something after having tasted a bite of the chili served in half of a ripe cantaloupe: "You call this chili hot!?" he asked.

"Oh, no sir, let me get you a bowl of our *hot* chili," came the response. When the waitress returned, our friend took one bite of his new serving of chili, turned almost purple and then broke out in a copious sweat.

"Is that hot enough for you, sir?" the waitress asked demurely.

"Fine," he choked out. Then, he slowly shoveled bite after painful bite into his face, trying to act as if he were eating ice cream. We not-so-sympathetic friends were laughing so hard at this point that we could easily have choked on our own chili, but to Bob's credit, he took it all in stride. Even though he was unable to talk for the rest of the evening, he ate every last spoonful of his chili. That is what I remember about Joann's Chili Bordello.

What Rita Baumgarten remembered is not that different from my memory of the Bordello on Atlantic Boulevard, located in the old Toddle House building. She said, "My dad, in his eighties, took Elayne Brown and me to lunch there one day. The waitresses wore bustiers over very short skirts. It was way ahead of Hooters for those days. We laughed so hard because the waitress knew my dad by his first name! It really was a 'for guys only' kind of place, although the food was good!"

Joann Perschel, who was the manager of the Chili Bordello, died in March 2009 of ovarian cancer. In her obituary, written by Charlie Patton in the *Florida Times Union* on March 18, 2009, it was noted that Joann was born in Syracuse, New York, and came to Jacksonville in the early '70s. She then learned the restaurant business by working in such places as Le Chateau and the Homestead Restaurant, and she spent her last decade working for the downtown Hilton.

Chili Bordello, with David Fletcher the center of attention. Joann Perschel is in the distance, standing. *Courtesy of David Fletcher.*

Chili Bordello scene. *Courtesy of David Fletcher.*

The obituary went on to say that Joann "managed Joann's Chili Bordello during the 1980s and 1990s, first on Atlantic Boulevard and later on Forsyth Street downtown. Reflecting her cheeky sense of humor, the decor was bordello red, Ms. Perschel dressed as a New Orleans madam, and the waitresses dressed in corsets and garter belts."

Such themed restaurants often hold interesting places in the hearts and minds of people who were lucky enough to get to eat in them. For me, however, I cannot help but remember poor Bob every time I sit down to a steaming bowl of chili, and I might even laugh a little. Maybe a lot.

THE SEA TURTLE AND THE GREEN TURTLE

Barry Adeeb, sixty-two and a graduate of Terry Parker High School and Florida State University, sat like royalty at one of his dining tables as his cleanup crew made his and Stan Jordan's diner ready for the next day's throng of customers while we talked. Beach's Diner, one of three in the franchise, is a wonderful dining experience located at 501 Atlantic Boulevard in Atlantic Beach, Florida. The bright white and blue décor sparkled in the afternoon sun as music of the '50s and '60s filled the air around us as we discussed Barry's life in the restaurant business and as part of one of the most successful family-run restaurant dynasties in the north Florida area.

From his earliest recollections, Barry recounted many fascinating details about how the members of his family were able to affect almost everyone in the area simply by being some of the finest restaurateurs in the business. He said that the Adeeb family had been in business for more than sixty years. It all began when Barry's grandfather, Joe Adeeb Sr., opened a hamburger place called the Three J's on Main Street in 1944, located where the Krystal's is now.

Joe Sr. then opened and operated the Green Turtle Restaurant on Philips Highway (US1), about half a mile south of the Jacksonville city limits. As a matter fact, the address was listed as "1/2 mile south on Philips Highway" in the 1960 telephone book.

The Green Turtle was a wonderful place where you could have a very fancy meal or where you could take clients to impress them. Although it did serve U.S. prime beef, it was, as the name implied, best known for

Barry Adeeb at his
Beach Diner. *Photo by
author.*

its "ocean fresh seafoods," as the postcard proclaimed. It catered "to the discriminating public."

D.H. Eaton shared a great memory about the Green Turtle:

> *My "older" boyfriend—twenty-one to my seventeen—was an Andrew Jackson graduate. He decided to escort me to my Englewood prom in 1966 but insisted we have dinner afterward at the Green Turtle on Philips Highway rather than the Sea Turtle at the Beach (where my classmates were all congregating for our prom breakfast). My "sophisticated" grown man boyfriend felt that a cozy elegant dining experience would be much more romantic. So we lobster'd and baked potato'd at the Green Turtle late into the night, just the two of us, sans my classmates, and I've been married to my "sophisticated" grown man boyfriend for forty-five years now, so his uptown sophistication must have worked.*

Green Turtle
Restaurant
on Philips
Highway.
*Courtesy of the
Florida State
Photographic
Archives.*

With the success of the Green Turtle, in about 1950, Joe Sr. then bought the Copper Kettle, a beachside restaurant and boardinghouse. He immediately changed the name to the Sea Turtle, and this enterprise, run primarily by his son, Joe Adeeb Jr., would eventually become the "crown jewel" in the Adeeb restaurant empire.

The forty-table Sea Turtle Restaurant was heavily damaged when Hurricane Dora swept into Jacksonville. Half of the dining room was destroyed and washed into the sea, but the Adeebs were not to be deterred. They kept the remaining part of the building open, about half the original's size, and in 1967, they were able to open an all-new restaurant. Only then would they allow the original to be demolished, so that there would not be one day of service lost.

Green Turtle postcard. *Courtesy of the Jacksonville Public Library's Florida Collection.*

In 1973, a two-hundred-room hotel was added to the restaurant, but it apparently opened at the height of the U.S. oil embargo during the Nixon administration. According to Barry, who was then right out of college with a degree in restaurant and hotel management:

> *It couldn't have been a worse time to open a hotel in a tourist location or to begin my career in the business as manager of the complex.*
>
> *George Bull, the developer of Selva Marina and Sevilla Condominiums, wanted to be the Sea Turtle Hotel's first overnight guest. He was not only that, but he was also the only guest. He stayed the second night, and when he came down the next morning, he asked me how it went. I said, "You're it!"*

Sea Turtle Hotel as seen from the air. *Courtesy of the Florida State Photographic Archives.*

We talked him into staying until we had some other guests. We also let him check out and stay in any room he wanted. We had the most stylish of color schemes—sixteen in all—and we wanted to show them off. Three nights later, we finally got some other company.

Sadly, with the building of Interstate 95, the Green Turtle slowly began to lose business, as did many other enterprises along Philips Highway. The Adeeb family closed this restaurant in 1975 when Joe Sr. died.

The Sea Turtle Hotel continued under Barry's management until 1997, when he retired, and the hotel was sold to One Ocean's. But all those years in the business must have influenced Barry more than he realized. He now spends his time running the diner on Atlantic Boulevard, with its better hours and less frantic pace.

For me, Sea Turtle Restaurant was the site of two celebrations in my life—my engagement and, several years later, the imminent birth of my first child.

Left: Sea Turtle matchbook.
Courtesy of Claire Fleming King

Below: Napkins from the Green Turtle and the Sea Turtle Restaurants. *Author items.*

For me, the Sea Turtle will always be very special, but how could it not be with the excellent food, the elegant atmosphere and the spectacular view of the ocean just beyond the windows.

It is interesting to note that Fred Abood, of Steer Room fame, is Barry's uncle. Joe Adeeb III, Barry's brother, is presently the owner of the ten Bono's Barbeque Restaurants in the Jacksonville area, working primarily at the Bono's near the St. Johns Town Center.

There can be no doubt that this family of restaurateurs has had a tremendous impact on the whole of Jacksonville's restaurant history—so much so that they are even very much part of the present.

OLD SOUTH RESTAURANT

When I think back on the Old South Restaurant, instantly I remember the wonderful vegetable plate special, served with cornbread and sweet iced tea. It rivaled my grandmother's fresh green beans cooked with bacon for special occasions. And just thinking about the Old South brings back thoughts of summer squash cooked with fresh onions, field peas and collard greens. For me, Old South was all about traditional southern cuisine, and I am hardly alone in my fond recollections of the place.

Patsy Butterbrodt, a retired educator who presently resides in Tennessee, has one outstanding memory of the Old South Restaurant, one of Jacksonville's most beloved eateries: "Every Sunday, after church, we would go to have Sunday dinner at the Old South Restaurant. And there were all these Baptists, Methodists, Lutherans and Presbyterians all going to the same place and all eating the same food. In my child eyes, I thought it very strange that all these theologically different people were somehow accepting their differences as they broke the same bread together...I also remember having to be very good. Children were not allowed to misbehave at all."

Patsy's mother, Irene Groth, a retired RN who once worked at Baptist Hospital, also thought very highly of the Old South Restaurant. "To me, it was a family-type place. You would see other families there. And the food was good, the service was good and the prices were good for families. All totaled, I suppose that is why we kept coming back. The Old South served basic food—no special meals or anything fancy."

Author D.H. Eaton said that what comes to her about the Old South Restaurant is nothing spectacular. "They did serve the most scrumptious crab cakes I have ever consumed anywhere. Perhaps those remarkable crab cakes were what kept me staying on as owner and manager of a beauty salon across the street from the restaurant for twenty years. When the Old South burned down, I decided I was burned out, too, and simply packed up and headed on out, burning my business bridges behind me."

Mendy Marks, a jewelry artist who lives in San Francisco, remembered the Old South very well. "The waitresses wore those scarf pins on their dresses, and they called you, 'honey.' I had lots of great fried chicken and shrimp there."

Anne Knight French, a retired guidance counselor, told me that "fried chicken, green beans and applesauce were some of my standard choices as a child when we went to the Old South. My father loved the coconut custard pie. Mother loved not cooking that night!"

"We often ate at the Old South Restaurant," said another native to the city, Candy Butler Solomon. "The Old South was in St. Nicholas, catty-corner to where Mudville Grill is now. It burned a few years ago but was where you could get a simple southern dinner."

According to a July 30, 1997 article in the *Florida Times-Union* written by staff writer Jim Schoettler, there was a predawn two-alarm fire at 5:30 a.m. that gutted the restaurant. At the time the restaurant burned, it was already fifty-five years old, and sadly, it was totally destroyed by a blaze blamed on faulty wiring. Mercedes Bell, a cook at the Old South for thirty-six years, was quoted in the article as saying, "We were like family. This is like a wake. I don't know what I'm going to do. I have to get over this first."

The article also said that the co-owner of the Old South, Talley George, seventy-nine, had just put the restaurant up for sale the week before in the hopes that he and his wife could soon retire. The other co-owner, Ralph Branch, who owned the building, said that he might rebuild. He never did.

It is not surprising to me that so many people remember the Old South so affectionately. Not only was there a wonderful array of comfort foods almost as good as grandma's cooking, but there was also a feeling of community built there. The article went on to quote Charlotte George, sixty-four, the wife of owner George, as saying, "Our customers were like family. We had generation after generation. It just meant so much to us."

If I hear people correctly, many of the patrons of the Old South had similar feelings.

CURB SERVICE DRIVE-INS

America's love of the automobile made for some very interesting developments in American culture, especially in the '50s and '60s. All over the country, there were drive-in movies, drive-in liquor stores and even drive-in funeral parlors, but the one kind of drive-in that was dear to most teenagers was the curb-service drive-in restaurants. Jacksonville was not immune to this "drive-in fever," and many very fine curb-service drive-ins popped up everywhere and became the backdrop of many an adolescence.

It was quite a treat to "hang out" at Bailey's, right across from Lee High School, or at the Texas Drive Inn near Landon High School. There was the Krystal's on Main Street and the one on Atlantic Boulevard, and there was Frisch's on Beach Boulevard. Pat's Drive Inn at the end of Normandy served teens their burgers and fries at their car windows, and Penny Burgers had two locations—one at the corner of Hershel and St. Johns and the other at Third Street at Jacksonville Beach. There was even a Milligan's.

The kids in Jacksonville embraced the *American Graffiti* lifestyle, and riding one's own souped-up car with a girl on your arm or your buddies in the back had to be the best ways to enjoy weekends, holidays and after-school leisure time.

Anne Knight French, a retired senior high guidance counselor, can remember very well an infamous place called the Texas Drive Inn. "It was on San Marco Boulevard, and the building was aqua. It had a dirt parking lot and was a major hangout for Landon High School students. I don't remember ever going in, as my big sister, a senior, would make me stay in the car!"

Another great story about the Texas Drive Inn, was told to me by longtime Jacksonville resident Pam Baker, a retired educator. "There was a big group of us girls who went to Landon and who were in the ninth grade," she said. "One time, my father dropped me off at a friend's house to a party where all of us girls were, and instead of having a party, we made it all the way to the beach, where we picked up some boys who came back with us to the Texas Drive Inn. What do you know? The word had gotten out that we girls were not where we were supposed to be, and our parents were waiting for us at the Texas. We were busted, and most of us spent the rest of the summer under restrictions. It really makes me laugh when I think about it now."

Steve Bishop, a native of Jacksonville and retired from the mortgage business, said, "I had dated the daughter of the owners of the Texas, Judy

Bailey's Drive Inn. *Courtesy of the Florida State Photographic Archives.*

Ekwurzel, and I went there for the out-of-this-world onion rings." High praise for a Westside boy.

Bishop's particular favorite drive-in was the Penny Burgers at Popular Point (the corner of St. Johns and Hershel). "It was owned by Bill Williams, and it was like an old-time Krystal's," he said. "It had fifteen-cent hamburgers, milkshakes, fries and cokes. You could drive in to a stall-like area—like Sonic has now—and carhops would come out and take your order. At one time, they came out on roller skates, but that was probably a bit too dangerous, so they went back to just walking…Eventually, they installed speakers like they had in drive-in movies. Penny Burgers was the place to hang out, though. That was the place where we all went to meet each other."

Longtime resident Barbara Lewis Milano remembered well her *American Graffiti* days. "It was like they made the movie just about us," she laughed. "Our destination of choice in the late '60s was the Krystal on Main Street. Usually, I went with a carload of girls, and even though it wasn't intended, we frequently would meet up with a carload of guys. It was great just sitting around and talking as waitresses would bring us our food on metal trays that they would hang on our car window. As I remember it, we might have exchanged a few phone numbers and all."

In homage to those long-ago days of curb service, Jacksonville has a monthly gathering of drivers in souped-up old cars who "cruise" down Main Street from First to Twelfth Streets, usually ending up at the new Krystal at 2023 Main Street, the old one no longer standing in the original location several blocks away.

The open-to-the-public rally takes place on the fourth Saturday of the month and draws quite a crowd of participants and onlookers. Some people dress in period clothes—poodle skirts and D.A. haircuts. And the selection of cars to see is quite varied—jalopies, Chevys, Carman Ghias, Volkswagens, Corvettes and more. Even motorcycles are represented. Every color of the rainbow is visible, and '50s and '60s music blares from car radios set to a special frequency specifically designed for this rally. The gathering is called the Historic Springfield Main Street Cruise.

Food vendors line the street, and many people set out their lawn chairs right next to their old cars as they enjoy the parade of vintage automobiles cruising up and down Main Street. Some people stroll from lot to lot looking at all the cars and talking with other participants about how things used to be. The whole experience truly captures the "glory days" spirit of a grown-up Jacksonville youth—the group that loved its drive-ins and the cars that drove them there.

PATTI'S ITALIAN AND AMERICAN RESTAURANT

Whenever I ask anyone what restaurant they remember from days past, the one place that came to mind most frequently was Patti's Italian and American Restaurant. My memory of Patti's is a bit hazy. I remember that the Division of Test Development and the Division of Accountability from the Duval County School Board were having a Christmas luncheon there, and as we prepared for our meal with a meditation, someone broke into the song "Let There Be Peace on Earth." I had to suppress a smile as I sang along, since the two divisions were so often at odds with each other. It did, however, make me aware that for the hour we spent together, we could be warmed by the season and the excellent food we were enjoying.

Patti's Italian and American Restaurant postcard. *Courtesy of the Jacksonville Public Library's Florida Collection.*

Patti's Italian and American Restaurant, at 7300 Beach Boulevard, was opened in 1951 by Peter and Mary Patti, and some years later, they set up a location at Roosevelt Mall. According to a November 27, 1967 article in the *Florida Times Union*, Mary learned her kitchen craft from her immigrant parents, and she was very proud of the fact that they only used family recipes. She was also very proud of the quality that went into all Patti's dishes.

"The seasoning is always added in precise amounts at the precise time. Our cooks are under strict instructions never to vary the routine," she said. "Of course, they are never to alter the recipe or substitute ingredients unless specifically asked to do so by the customer." That is probably why customers kept coming back—great food all the time. But they also came back because they felt at home. "Many of our customers have been with us so long that I remember when they used to have to sit in a high chair…We want people to always feel as though they were sitting in their own home. If a child knocks over a glass of milk, we don't want anyone to feel embarrassed."

The Pattis were also very careful about the employees they hired, because as Mrs. Patti said, "A discourtesy or an oversight by a waitress can ruin the taste of the best meal ever prepared…It's only human nature, and we try

Top: Patti's Italian and American Restaurant matchbook. *Courtesy of Barbara Lewis Milano.*

Bottom: Patti's Italian and American Restaurant drink token. *Courtesy of Claire Fleming King.*

to do everything possible to avoid this. You wouldn't stay in business long if you didn't."

Patti's Restaurant also did a booming business with its fine takeout service. It sold sauces by the pint or gallon so that customers could make good meals at home. Eventually, it began to prepare prepackaged frozen meals that were indistinguishable from meals served at the restaurant.

D.H. Eaton recalled this about Patti's: "Early in our marriage—probably circa 1968–75—we were regular Patti's customers, especially for takeouts from that cubbyhole room on the side of the building. You waited for your food order to come out while seated on what appeared to be an old car seat. And no matter how many times you sat there on that bunged-up old seat, you never tired of staring at, and talking about, the boxed array of every shape of pasta noodles known to man that was stacked around the perimeter of the room on shelves."

Jan Glassman currently lives in Jacksonville and is an administrative assistant at River Garden Hebrew Home. She said, "Our family used to eat at Patti's practically every Sunday night. Our waitress knew exactly what each one of us was going to order, even knowing that the vegetarians in the family would want the side spaghetti with marinara sauce rather than the regular spaghetti sauce, which had meat in it. Only problem was that many years later, we were informed by another waitress that Patti's marinara sauce was made with sausage. Most of our family would never eat meat at restaurants due to keeping kosher, but oh well!"

Margaret Rose, who retired after thirty-one years with the State of Florida and who currently lives in Mandarin, said, "Patti's was my favorite…that was our go-to restaurant for birthdays and other celebrations. When Patti's closed, Chef Patti went to work for Sysco."

Of course, the most-loved dish served at Patti's was the boneless chicken parmigiana, and many people have been trying to duplicate the recipe ever since. Ivy Ludwig Eyrick considers herself an expert on Patti's since each of her two children was born the day after a night at Patti's. "There were many people who have tried to figure out how to make Patti's Parmesan chicken (although there really isn't any Parmesan in it—only provolone and mozzarella). First, you do not flatten or pound the chicken. You cook it in bread crumbs in the oven, and then they use a sauce that no one can duplicate…I do remember that when it was a person's birthday, they would bring you a slice of pizza with a sparkler in it. It was a great place to go!"

Only Alvin Brown, former Jacksonville resident who now lives in New York, had anything unflattering to say about Patti's. "Patti's was our go-to Italian restaurant. Sunday nights we would go there, as well as for special occasions, for spaghetti and meatballs. Until I lived in New York and spent time in Italy, I did not realize that Italy had a lot of other kinds of food and realized how bad Patti's actually was!"

I suppose for those of us who didn't know any better, Patti's was what Italian food was all about. The friendly service and warm, welcoming atmosphere certainly made up for any lack of sophistication Patti's may have suffered. We just loved the place.

LE CHATEAU

In the realm of sophistication, Jacksonville and the north Florida area have traditionally entertained a rather "provincial" reputation. This place is not the epicenter of fashion or music or societal trends, but it certainly has had its share of classy eating establishments. Le Chateau once reigned at Atlantic Beach at Seventh and Ocean Front Drive, and it was one of the very finest restaurants.

Le Chateau was a glamorous place. It wasn't the type of place where middle-class families took the kids out for a hamburger. It was for very special occasions. My parents went to Le Chateau maybe once a year for their anniversary, and they were dressed almost formally when they drove off. Le Chateau was the kind of place where high school juniors and seniors would take their dates before their proms; and it was certain to be the place where sumptuous wedding receptions could make a couple's life together get off on the right foot.

According to a March 3, 1985 article by R. Michael Anderson in the *Florida Times-Union*, the Spanish-Mediterranean building was originally a mansion built in 1937 by Haydn W. Crosby. This mansion remained a private residence until it was sold to Gary Adams, who turned the building into the Atlantic Beach Club in 1944. Adams later sold it to a man who rented the building out as a summer home. Then, in 1954, Bill Maze bought the property and turned the site into Le Chateau. In 1959, Preben Johansen purchased the property and turned it into an elegant restaurant, one of the most legendary places in our area.

On a beautiful May morning, I sat down with two very important people in Johansen's life: his wife, Nina Hazelhurst Johansen, and their daughter,

Beach side of Le Chateau. *Courtesy of Kathy Johansen Marvin.*

Kathy J. Marvin and Nina Johansen. *Photo by author.*

Kathy Johansen Marvin. The spring sunshine filtered down onto us as we sat in a patio of Lillie's Coffee Bar at Neptune Beach. We were but a few miles from the property that once held the elegant Le Chateau.

Nina told me all about her life before Le Chateau. When World War II ended, Nina and a bunch of her friends spent a year in Munich, Germany, to be stenographers. "It really was a great adventure! I left St. Petersburg, Florida, and found myself helping to pursue Nazi war criminals. There was a dance hall nearby with a big band and all, and that is where I met my future husband, Preben. He was such a wonderful dancer—he could waltz and tango. He knew all the dances, and I loved dancing!"

Johansen was a Dane who worked as a translator for the U.S. government at that time, and Nina said that when she returned to the States, she just couldn't get over him. So, she went back over to Germany and "got him." They were married in Europe, and she said that his parents were wonderful to her.

When the Johansens came back to Florida, Preben worked at the Sea Turtle Restaurant under the tutelage of Joe Adeeb, the owner. There he learned his trade as restaurateur. He began as a dishwasher, and he worked his way up to manager. It wasn't too much longer in 1959 that he bought Le Chateau, and using what he had learned at the Sea Turtle, he turned the place into a real gem.

Kathy Marvin, who worked for her father for thirteen years, remembered many of those wonderful times of Le Chateau:

> The days of Le Chateau were a totally different era—it was a time of our four-piece band or Gene Nordan singing at the piano. It was a time when people really dressed up to go out, wore tuxes. They came to Le Chateau to get engaged or celebrate anniversaries or birthdays. And we did it up in style. Our most popular dish was Steak Diane, [which] we prepared at the table along with our salads. For dessert, we might bring out a flaming baked Alaska, or we might prepare Cherries Jubilee or Bananas Foster at your seat. And all our wines were French until we came to realize the California wines were better. Yes, it was a very different time.

Marvin had a few wonderful celebrity stories. Victor Borges was always a guest at Le Chateau when he was in Jacksonville. He and Preben would have many conversations in Danish, their native language. Barry Goldwater was also a memorable guest, and Prince Andrew once came to escape the media when he was in the area.

Preben and Nina Johansen. *Courtesy of Kathy Johansen Marvin.*

But nothing was as exciting as when Harry Kissinger called Julie and David Eisenhower when they were dining at Le Chateau. Of course, the Secret Service was all around, but it really was a sight when these two were escorted through the hot, busy kitchen to the office of Marvin's father to take the phone call.

Another tidbit that Marvin recounted concerned Liberace. Apparently, he was very fond of Le Chateau and often went there after concerts—that is, until people realized that Marvin's father secretly held the place open for Liberace. He had to stop coming because other people began to come and expect a concert. He just wanted to relax, and he wasn't able to deal with the press of people that began to arrive. But before things got out of hand, Liberace had dinner there often, and then he would go into the piano bar with Marvin's father and mother. Once Betty Grable joined them.

One of the best parts of the whole Le Chateau experience was listening to Gene Nordan sing and play the piano for the patrons. I was fortunate enough to get to visit with him as well on a different day at Lilly's. Nordan was the pianist at Le Chateau for thirteen years, and presently, he plays piano at six different country clubs and ten retirement communities. He has

Left: Gene Nordan. *Photo by author.*

Below: The Kalkines family dining at Le Chateau. *From left to right*: Anne Costos, Gia Gia (pronounced *yia yia*), Chris Kalkines, George Costos, Gus Costos, Lillian Costos, Jeanette Kalkines, Harry Kalkines and Kathy Kalkines. *Courtesy of Kathy Kalkines Rhodes.*

a six-month gig beginning in May at Linville Ridge Resort in Grandfather Mountain, North Carolina, and he plays once a month at his church and for private parties. He had many great stories about celebrities for whom he played his piano.

One of the best stories Nordan told was about Liberace: "On a cold February night after Liberace had performed at the Civic Auditorium, he came late to Le Chateau for dinner. When the place was closed, Liberace and I retired to La Dora Lounge, where I played for 'the master' until five in the morning. For a while after, we wrote letters back and forth. My wife thought he was collecting stories to tell during his concerts."

Nordan also told a story about taking George Hamilton to an American Cancer Society benefit in his very ordinary Chevy. And he told a wonderful story about Mamie Van Doren. "I took my break one night when Mamie Van Doren was a guest at Le Chateau. She asked me to reach under the table to feel how toned her legs were. She was indeed very fit, as was my imagination," he said.

And then there was the time a patron was so intoxicated that he passed out in the back of a pickup truck in their parking lot. Poor guy found himself the next morning in Fernandina.

Le Chateau had entertained many other notables—Taylor Caldwell, Pernell Roberts and Jane Russell, just to name a few. But many other less famous but no less important patrons were the local people who have lovely memories made at Le Chateau.

Ponte Vedra resident Kathy Kalkines Rhodes, who has never moved from the north Florida area, recalled one of her fondest memories. "I'm pretty sure the first time I 'slow danced,' I danced with my brother at Le Chateau. When we finished, the bandleader asked the audience to 'give the little couple a hand!' We always took our out-of-town company there to enjoy dinner and dancing. The restaurant had a photographer floating around taking pictures. I have a photo of our family that was taken from one of these occasions."

Lanese Hartley, who grew up in Mandarin, remembered Le Chateau in this way: "Le Chateau was a prom night destination. It was way out of my usual price range back then! It was also my first exposure to French cuisine. I was at Le Chateau for their New Years Eve party in 1967, and in 1968, I kissed with the guy who eventually became my husband. It was a special place for me!"

But a place with such wonderful stories is not immune to the misfortunes of life. When Hurricane Dora swept through north Florida in September

Postcard of Le Chateau. *Courtesy of Kathy Johansen Marvin.*

1964, Le Chateau was devastated. The ocean swamped the dining room, which then literally fell into the sea. Most of the entire complex was in ruins. But out of those ruins came a symbol of resiliency.

Nordan told me, "The story goes that when they were going through the debris, a bronze hand stuck out of a pile of sand. It was the arm of the bronze statue of a Greek woman holding an urn on her shoulder. The Johansens were so happy to have found her that they renamed her La Dora, for the storm, and they placed her in the center of the patio during the renovations. They also renamed the bar La Dora Lounge."

The 1985 *Times-Union* article said that Johansen got a federal disaster loan and had the restaurant renovated with a larger dining room, a new bar, a patio filled with tropical plants and a new spiral staircase that led up to an upstairs banquet room.

According to Marvin, her father acquired the Homestead Restaurant in 1962 and was able to keep his businesses afloat while Le Chateau was being renovated. He would sell the Homestead to the Macri family in 1975.

Mr. Johansen was quite a force of nature, according to Mr. Nordan. "He pumped gas, sold shoes, worked at the Sea Turtle as a dishwasher and then became manager there. When opportunity knocked, he bought Le Chateau and turned it into something wonderful. Later, he was a city councilman for

Chandelier from Le Chateau.
Courtesy of Gene Nordan.

Atlantic Beach and the mayor of the city. He also became a pilot and even represented Atlantic Beach on the Jacksonville City Council at one time. He was short, but he had a very powerful presence. Mr. Personality."

Sadly, all good things must come to an end. The restaurant continued for three years after the death of Mr. Johansen in 1983. Nina sold the property in 1985 to Dan Crisp, who was to build condos at that location. Marvin explained that because of the restaurant's location in a residential area, it made it hard to continue. As old neighbors moved out and new ones came in, there was less acceptance of parking and noise issues that come with thriving restaurant businesses, so the property was sold and the old building destroyed.

Nordan remembered that sad time, saying, "When Channel 4 came to film the demolition of Le Chateau, I had tears in my eyes as I watched. I was only able to salvage two chandeliers, and both are now hanging in my house. But my years working at Le Chateau represented the 'golden age' of my youth,' but I was too green to know it."

I suppose we were all too green to realize that a place like Le Chateau could not last forever. Thankfully, many of us were able to enjoy its food, its ambiance and the wonderful people who drifted in and out of its rooms and patios. Le Chateau memories are always quite special.

THE HOMESTEAD RESTAURANT

The Homestead Restaurant was an important part of the beach community for many decades, and I learned about that when I was given access to a twenty-two-year-old menu with a short history of the place. It said that the two-story, pine log building was constructed in 1932 at 1712 Beach Boulevard. Before its use as the restaurant, it was the residence of Mrs. Alpha O. Payner, who used it as a rooming house. Although it didn't say it, Mrs. Payner was a fabulous cook. And so began the legend of one of the most beloved restaurants in the area.

In 1962, Payner sold the Homestead to Preben Johansen of Le Chateau fame, and ownership eventually passed to the Macri family in 1975. In 2002, Kathy Johansen Marvin and her husband, Malcolm, bought the place from Carmen Macri. The Marvins eventually sold the place to Hank Woodburn, who owned Adventure Landing. He leased the property to several others who tried to make a go of it, but road/bridge construction issues on Beach Boulevard proved too much. Woodburn sold the old Homestead location to Don and Debbie Nichol, who opened Tacolu Baja Mexicana in November 2012.

Homestead Restaurant sign.
Courtesy of John Hull.

98

I sat down one hot summer afternoon with Larry Gordon and Jennifer Wannamaker, both of whom worked many years at the Homestead. If I learned anything about the Homestead from them, it was that the Homestead served as a gathering place for all kinds of people from all different social levels, and the service made each and every patron feel welcome and at home.

Jennifer said, "We all cared about one another at the Homestead, and when it was about to be closed after the Macri family sold it, many people came and would literally break down as they said their goodbyes. We had opened early so people at funerals across the street could come and celebrate the life of the departed. People got engaged there, celebrated getting pregnant and it was where generation after generation of families came to feed their children."

Larry agreed with Jennifer. "It was a very special place, to be sure, but it also had really great food. Dan Jenkins had written an article about us in *Golf Digest* about how PGA Tour participants often dined with us."

Jennifer added, "And we had been featured in *Southern Living* magazine a number of times as well. We even had chefs come from Disney World to try to learn how to make our cat's head biscuits. I don't think they ever got it right."

And then there were the ghost stories. Larry's story went like this: "I was cleaning up as we were closing down one night. There was a fireplace in the middle of the room that opened on both sides. I see out of the corner of my eyes a puff of smoke. I figured it was a napkin a patron might have thrown in the fire igniting on the dying coals, so I go around to the other side, and there she was: a lady in a long, white dress and a veil over her face. I was shocked, to say the least, and I looked away to see if anyone else was seeing this, and when I looked back, she and the smoke were gone."

Jennifer's stories were many—from hearing children playing as she was working up in the office to falling off a chair only to have something push her back to safety, but her overall sense of the ghostly happenings was that "the presences there seemed to me to be benevolent, and they always made me feel safe and protected."

After my interview, I asked some friends if they had any stories about the Homestead. Elaine Pennywitt Danese, a resident of Mandarin and a court reporter, told me, "I once asked the manager at the Homestead if there were any ghosts there, and she told me that there weren't any, but many strange things had happened whenever they went to turn on their alarm system. She also said that one of the waitresses had been setting up for the next day when she heard voices, and there was no one there but her."

Michael Fogg, who still lives at Atlantic Beach, e-mailed me his Homestead Restaurant experience. It occurred in the early '70s, when he and his surfer-hippie friends visited every Saturday night:

> *In those days there were two things: All you can eat Fried Chicken, for $1.50, and all you can eat Fried Shrimp for $2.00. Of course, this also included creamed peas, mashed potatoes, and home-made biscuits. I think ice tea was extra.*
>
> *Being gentlemen, we would ALWAYS bring enough money for a suitable tip for a waitress who we would completely abuse with many return trips to the kitchen for refills of everything. We ate until we could not possibly eat any more. Then, exhausted and satisfied beyond comprehension, we would fall back into my car, digging for change to see if we could pool enough money for a six pack of beer on the way home.*
>
> *Then, one day, tragedy struck. As we followed our Saturday ritual to the letter, everything in life seemed normal and perfect. I think we even said the blessing, in anticipation, as we made the drive to the Homestead. After mowing our way through the first serving, we were almost instinctively holding up our plates with cries of "More Chicken, please," "A few more biscuits," etc. There was a dull silence. We thought we were in trouble or something.*
>
> *As the manager approached our table, we became almost paranoid. He addressed us as "Gentlemen" (this couldn't be good), "I regret to inform you, but the Homestead is no longer on an 'All you can eat' basis menu. You receive one serving, and one serving only."*
>
> *Life, and the quality thereof, has never been the same since.*

I suppose the same could have been said when the old Homestead closed for good. Life at the beach and the quality thereof has never been the same since.

PART III
Everywhere Else

DENNY MORAN'S, BAMBOO LUAU AND KARL HELLENTHAL'S RESTAURANTS

On October 31, 1976, an article ran in the *Florida Times-Union* about a strip of highway on the Westside with businesses that were extremely lucrative. The article was titled "Restaurant Row: A Westside Phenomenon," and John Peters, the *Time-Union* business editor wrote, "Steaks, burgers, tacos, chicken, lobster and rice. This is part of what's cooking along a two mile strip of Blanding Boulevard—a stretch of road dubbed 'restaurant row.'"

Partly because it was nestled between two major naval installations— the Naval Air Station Jacksonville and Naval Air Station Cecil Field—this stretch of highway was poised to acquire the income of navy personnel, so much so that budgets reflected it when the air stations had their paydays.

From Cedar River to 103rd Street, there were twenty nationally named franchised restaurants and five independent ones. Customers could spend anywhere from $1.25 to $8.00 for meals along this strip, and Fred Levy, a co-owner of the Bamboo Luau said in the article, "I'd conservatively say the restaurants here do $10 to $12 million in business in a year."

All of this was to confirm what many Westside baby boomers have told me many times: when they ate out, they mostly went to fast-food establishments.

They had neither the time nor the money to go to really fancy places far from their neighborhoods. I am also sure that naval personnel were not so much into fine dining as they were into fast food and happy hours.

However, there were three restaurants that were consistently mentioned when I spoke with Jacksonville Westsiders about when they went out to eat at fancier places. Two were located on this strip of Blanding Boulevard. They were Denny Moran's and the Bamboo Luau on Cedar Creek. The third, Karl Hellenthal's, was not too much farther away on Normandy Boulevard. Each restaurant added a special kind of culinary flair to the dining experience of those living out west and to those who would venture over there for excellent food.

Denny Moran's operated at 2509 Blanding Boulevard and liked to call itself "the family steakhouse." The *Florida Times-Union* on January 17, 1970, ran a review about Denny Moran's that said the place, "was designed and built especially for dining pleasure and convenience."

As it continued, the article noted that Denny Moran prided himself at being able to serve a complete, made-to-order steak dinner to each customer within ten minutes of arriving at the door. The menu was on the wall in the "serving alcove," where a customer would choose a dinner. He or she would then be given a ticket before even being seated. Then, the customer gets to select a table in one of the large dining areas, where a waitress would take drink orders and bring salads. The article noted that "within six to eight minutes, the waitress brings your entrée, broiled to perfection according to your specifications, on a hot sizzling platter."

Linda Gable Beckham, a longtime Westside resident, said, "Denny Moran's was great. I was in D.C.T. [diversified cooperative training] my senior year. We sent invitations to our employers and had our 'end of the year' banquet at Denny Moran's. I felt so grown up and was so proud to have my boss with me at our dinner. And I remember the stuffed mushrooms at Denny's were so incredibly delicious! Sometimes we'd run by and pick up several orders and build a meal around them."

Lynn Curtis knew a great deal about Denny Moran's. She had worked for Mr. Moran for several years:

> *I worked for Denny at three locations, including operation of his ice cream shop, Lil Aubrey's, named for his daughter. Denny Moran adopted his famous house salad from Fred Abood of the Green Derby Restaurant on Riverside Avenue, a Steer House–type of restaurant. Of course, Denny never had the opportunity to open his new restaurant on the water. He had*

started to have business problems and had to close the place. He moved out of town for a few years, then returned to open a place called Salty's. He and his wife came up with the name Salty's while traveling back this way when they saw a billboard that had an old sailor on it and the words "Old Salty."

His wife, Sharon, worked for him before they married. And Denny had lots of interests—he loved to fly his plane. I also remember that he was one of the best joke tellers around. But he was also a genuinely nice guy. I've seen him give food to down-and-out people who would come to the takeout window. He was really great.

In July 1989, Denny Moran's was padlocked by the Internal Revenue Service for nonpayment of taxes, according to the *Florida Times-Union* on August 5, 1989. In the article, Moran attributed his financial problems to "an underfinanced mortgage on a new riverfront addition in 1987. Moran said he hopes to reopen after selling his property to Cedar River Seafood and Oyster Bar." Moran was also quoted as saying, "If they buy, we plan to lease from them and reopen in our old place and they will open the new addition on the river. We would not sell seafood, but would be a steak house."

It is interesting that Buddy Ross, who told me a story about Biser's Restaurant earlier, was the finance officer who helped Denny Moran resolve his money problems with the IRS. Eventually, Moran settled his accounts, with the guidance from Ross, and he and his wife were then eventually able to open a place called Salty's on Lane Avenue.

Denny Moran died on July 30, 1999, after a lengthy illness. He was well remembered for his devotion to family and to his forty-year legacy in the restaurant business.

THERE WAS SOMETHING about a restaurant that attempted to be a little piece of a Polynesian paradise right there at 3488 Blanding Boulevard. By Jacksonville standards, Bamboo Luau was a very exotic place.

Susie Ross, a retired nurse and longtime resident of the Westside, said, "When I first went to Bamboo Luau, I felt like a kid in a candy store. My mouth must have dropped when I saw women servers rather skimpily dressed, in Hawaiian fashion, and the men didn't wear shirts either. I had never been to anything like this before. It was so new and exciting, and the food was terrific."

Trishia Richards Repp Parker, a business analyst living near Tampa, had a different take on the restaurant. She had been a waitress at Bamboo

Luau right after graduation from Florida State University in 1972. "Wow, 'Bamboo Luau' and 'fine restaurant' just doesn't click in my head. It was a Polynesian food restaurant, most of which I didn't like. My memory is of the management and how awful they were to the staff. The manager delighted in getting at least one waitress crying or it didn't seem to be a good night for him. I was a terrible waitress and couldn't tell one dish from another, so I was always giving the wrong dish to the wrong person. That was my last waitress job. To the rest of the world, it must have been a fun place to eat because they were always very busy."

Even if the waitstaff was far from happy, customers still flocked there to enjoy, as their business directory advertisements said, "Polynesian Delights, Live Maine Lobster, Fresh Seafoods, and Prime Cuts of Beef."

One very interesting tidbit of information came to me from Bart Parramore, a Jacksonville native. "Supposedly, Elvis Presley would always go to Bamboo Luau while in town because he had an army buddy that worked there—a chef, I believe. Just a story I used to hear, but I can't confirm it."

Even if Bart could not confirm the story, Pama Lee Herlong, also of the Westside, shared a story that made his information more plausible. "If I am not mistaken, Fred and Sandy Levy were co-owners of the Bamboo Luau with Gilbert and Marianne Makoul, although Fred may have been a manager. One of them got the insider passes to Elvis shows from Dee Presley, Elvis's stepmother, who was always hanging out at the Bamboo Luau when she was in town visiting her son. Fred always had a slide show running on a screen in the lounge of an after-show party they all attended with Elvis in a Hilton Suite."

The Bamboo Luau was also a happening place for reasons other than Elvis and its "Sneaky Tiki Cocktail." Donald Smith of the Westside said, "I remember Bamboo Luau. It was Prichard's Kitchen before being Bamboo Luau. We went many times as kids since they had an all-you-could-eat special. I also remember going to a fish fry that Claude Kirk held during his run for governor. Good times." The good times there came to an end in either 1977 or 1978. After 1977, Bamboo Luau is no longer listed in the Jacksonville business directory.

As I was often told, Karl Hellenthal's Restaurant was a wonderful treat, and it was one of the premier restaurants of Jacksonville in the '50s, '60s and early '70s. John Hill, retired from the Army National Guard and a Jacksonville resident, remembered most fondly his times at Karl Hellenthal's Restaurant:

The restaurant was located on Blanding across from Normandy Mall, and the building there is still standing. It was a very fancy place to me. It had a dark interior with wood paneling. I remember it very well.

On September 12, 1973, I went there twice in one day. First, I went there to help celebrate my parents' twenty-fifth wedding anniversary at the lunch hour. Then, we went back there for dinner when my cousin arrived later in the day.

The specialty of the house was a broiled shrimp and crab casserole, and the restaurant was well known for its salads made at tableside.

Paulette Reiger Sikes remembered that they always had live music at Hellenthal's, mostly piano. "Whenever I went there as a kid, my little brother would get a Davey Crockett and I would get a Shirley Temple."

Linda Frigo McDaris said, "Karl Hellenthal's was a family-run restaurant, and they had the best fried green tomatoes. Actually, everything on their menu was delicious. I went to school with the owner's son, David. He had one of the little cars that you could drive on land or water."

Paul Dixon of the Westside also remembered Hellenthal's very well. "We always had a bottle of their French salad dressing in the 'fridge.' One bit of family lore says that on the night I was born, my mother and father had been out eating at Hellenthal's. Mom always said she had a huge meal that night, which, er, helped ease me into the world!"

Another Westside resident, Julie Owen, told me, "My rehearsal dinner was held at Karl Hellenthal's in 1978. I recall meeting the owner; her husband had passed away, and she was going to close the restaurant. I moved away so don't know when the restaurant closed."

Hellenthal's actually closed in 1979.

THE PALMS FISH CAMP AND THE BUCCANEER RESTAURANT

Whenever I have out-of-town company, I love to take them through the real Florida, and I can do that best by driving Heckscher Drive north to Fernandina. There are wetlands and beaches, palm trees and overhanging oaks, all of which are amazingly beautiful. The variety of scenes that make up my route makes me wonder what the first Europeans thought when they began to explore this area.

Art Jennette cooking. *Photo by author.*

Not long after I cross the Dames Point Bridge and turn toward the north, a restaurant lies quietly closed and ready for a buyer at 6359 Heckscher Drive. The Palm Fish Camp was once a thriving ramshackle place where Art Jennette, the master of the "Art of Cracker Cooking," became a legend.

If ever there was a person who loved his job, Art is that person. Thankfully, he is still working his magic at a place called Checker Bar-B-Q on St. Augustine Road. To watch him do his work is like watching a complete ballet. He synchronizes his motions as he fries tomatoes, shrimp and chicken and then swiftly turns to flip slabs of barbeque on the grill. It is like watching Mikhail Baryshnikov float across a stage. And this "dance" occurs as Art calls out in a gravelly voice, "Fryin' the chicken!" or "Frying the tomatoes!" Then, before you know it, he is hobnobbing with the customers, making sure that plates are loaded with his best dishes and all the glasses are filled to the brim with beverages.

Go back a decade or so, and this dance would have occurred at a very different place on the Northside of Jacksonville. The Palms was a beloved institution that operated on the edge of a swamp right off Heckscher Drive. It had originally been a fish camp owned by Jennette's mother and stepfather, and with what Art had learned from his mother about cooking, he was able to turn the Palms into one of the most celebrated eateries in the area.

Art, who was the life and soul of the Palms, was born in Springfield and went to school at Oakhill Elementary, Jeff Davis, and was a graduate of Forrest High School, class of 1972. His culinary skills he acquired from his mother and aunts, who came from Alma, Georgia, and were "farm girls come to the big city." He also learned a great deal from John Wright at the Westside Skill Center and gained a good bit of experience by being in the restaurant business from a very early age. He was sixteen when he started at Burger King, but before long, he was the youngest manager ever at a Bonanza Steakhouse.

When his mother and stepfather bought the Palms Fish Camp, Art worked there while he catered to such places as the River Club and some of the party boats. Before too long, he was getting noticed for "cooking the food he grew up with." Then he was pulling in all kinds of customers, from neighborhood folks to the more celebrated people of prominence.

Jake Godbold, the mayor of Jacksonville from 1978 to 1987, had been a frequent patron, as was Ander Crenshaw, U.S. congressman representing District 4 of Jacksonville, at least whenever he was in town.

According to Art, the City of Jacksonville leased the place to his stepfather, but eventually there was a dispute about the quality of the condition of the property. It was condemned, but because so many people, politicians included, frequented the place and because of the lively antics of the host, the Palms continued for many years until it was finally forced to close down.

Ron Littlepage of the *Times-Union* even wrote about it in his column on January 30, 2013. He noted:

> *The Palms Fish Camp was a popular, albeit grubby, dining spot on Heckscher Drive next to Clapboard Creek.*
>
> *When it closed in 2005, the city purchased the property to make improvements to the boat ramp there and to add much-needed parking.*
>
> *An additional idea—not a bad one at the time—was to enter into an agreement with a private company to re-create the Palms to return a*

fish camp atmosphere, although not so grubby this time, to the edge of the Timucuan preserve.

Seven years later, the building is there, but it's empty and fried shrimp and fish aren't being served. Instead today's menu only contains lawsuits.

Thankfully, all the hubbub has not deterred Art Jennette from being the premier cracker chef in this area. So, all you need for a dinner and a show is to head down to Checker Bar-B-Q on Old St. Augustine Road, not far from Emerson Street. If you enter into this very unassuming space, don't be fooled. Soon you will be pampered with service and fed some of the finest southern cooking there ever was. I'm telling you, you cannot beat any of it with a stick.

If I were to continue my scenic Florida travels down Heckscher Drive, just about the time I get to the Kingsley Plantation, with the ferry launch across the street, I am reminded that there once was a fabulous eating establishment nearby called Buccaneer Seafood. It once stood at 9636 Heckscher Drive and has since been totally replaced by a business called Resource Plus.

According to Ben Worthington, a retired electrician who now lives in what he calls "God's country" (Cleveland, Georgia), the old Buccaneer Seafood Restaurant was one of the best. He said that it was a large, somewhat shabby, white clapboard building with a tin roof. Since the early '50s, it had been located on the Heckscher Drive side of the Ferry crossing.

"One of the best parts of the Buccaneer was this old guy with a big white beard who stood at the front door and welcomed the customers with great seafaring stories. He wore this navy blue Greek captain's hat with white shirt and dress pants, and he looked like he had just stepped off the boat. His name was Captain McGraw, and he entertained everyone with tales of the sea."

Worthington recalled that the Buccaneer was a BYOB restaurant, where you brought your own alcoholic beverages since they didn't have a liquor license, and that there were the obligatory nets and glass balls on the walls as decoration.

"Best of all was the fresh-caught seafood and the Whaler Platter that was more food than two people could eat. It had flounder, snapper, grouper, shrimp, clams, oysters, stuffed crab shells and filet mignon with baked potatoes. And before all of that, there was a shrimp cocktail. It cost twenty-eight dollars, and it was huge. You always had food to take home."

Erick Mixer, another Jacksonville native, said that he and his friends would "get our food there and drive to the jetties when you could go in by the bridge on low tide around the lagoon and park."

Buccaneer matchbook. *Courtesy of Claire Fleming King.*

Donna Richie Pitts, also of Jacksonville, said, "The Buccaneer was our Friday night out-to-dinner place for years! Only place my stepdad would take us. I had my first shrimp dinner there and have loved it ever since."

I can only imagine the wonders that would have been mine had I ever gotten the chance to sit in such an entertaining restaurant, eating great seafood and watching the Florida landscape unfold around me: the ferry

109

carrying commuters and their cars across the water and the wildlife slithering or swooping nearby—all this while being entertained by an old salt's stories.

THE THUNDERBIRD MOTOR HOTEL

I have no memory of the Thunderbird Motor Hotel or any of the four lounges that were within its walls—the Zodiac Room, the Wonderfall, the Terrace Room and the King's Inn. The Thunderbird was in its heyday when I was too young to go into it. Still, it was one of Jacksonville's most "happening" places, which is why I have included it in my list of lost restaurants.

"I certainly remember the Thunderbird," said Donna Stein McNett, longtime Jacksonville resident and an interior designer.

My father, Albert Stein, conceived the idea of the Thunderbird Hotel and Supper Club and built it…My dad and his two brothers—Martin Stein, who developed Regency Mall, and David Stein, who ran Burger King—were always inspired by their father, my grandfather, Ben Stein. Prior to opening the Thunderbird, my grandfather invested in what is now Burger King. My uncle, David Stein, the only surviving son of Ben Stein, continued with Burger King for many years.

My dad built the Thunderbird when I was growing up, and I got to have my sweet sixteen birthday luncheon there, but to tell you the truth, I can't remember much about it except that I had a bunch of my friends for lunch, and we all dressed up. I'm sure it was "girls only."

We also used to go to the Supper Club that had some pretty big-name entertainment and for its time was a pretty big deal for Jacksonville. We're going back to 1964 to 1965. I remember once one of the entertainers was going to come to our house for dinner. Her name was Yvonne Moray. I was not told anything about her except where and when to pick her up at the Hotel. So, I'm waiting and waiting, and I keep hearing this tapping on the side of my car. But I don't see anyone. So, I get out, and low and behold, a midget women is there. She had played a munchkin in The Wizard of Oz.

Alvin Brown, now living in New York, had this to say about the Thunderbird: "My dad was a regular at the Thunderbird, since everyday

Thunderbird sign. *Courtesy of Donna Stein McNett*.

Poolside at the Thunderbird Motor Hotel, with Albert Stein, the owner, sitting in the shade. *Courtesy of Donna Stein McNett.*

The Wonderfall Room at the Thunderbird Motor Hotel. *Courtesy of Donna Stein McNett.*

he would stop off there for a drink before he went home. When it was time for my bar mitzvah, my parents held the party at the Robert Meyer Hotel downtown. It was a bigger affair than was usual for the Jacksonville Jewish community—many guests, a candle-lighting service and a big cake. We had the Robert Meyer booked until midnight, then everyone went back to the Thunderbird, where my out-of-town guests were staying. The party continued at the pool until 3:00 in the morning!"

For Judy Greenfield, a longtime Jacksonville resident who is presently retired, the Thunderbird was a very special place: "The Thunderbird was where we spent our wedding night. It was brand new and we had room no. 11. It was so new that they didn't have a restaurant yet, so we went across the street to the Howard Johnson to collect ourselves after the wedding. The waitress asked if I had just got married. And I said yes, but how could she tell? And she said, 'You have rice in your hair.' The fact that I was all dressed up in my new going-away dress wasn't a giveaway, now was it?"

According to Chris Kalkines, a consulting psychologist:

> *The Atter sisters were quite prominent singers around town in the late 1950s and early 1960s. They were both single, pretty and could sing like it was nobody's business. Virginia went on to become famous on local TV, and when I was very young, she held me on her lap and sang a song to me on live TV. (They needed a young male child for a prop, and my dad just happened to have one who would work for free.) She sang on* The Jimmy Strickland Show, *which was sponsored by Copeland's Sausage, and Copeland's was one of my dad's accounts. He sold TV advertising for WJXT, Channel 4. Virginia's sister, who I never met, apparently was a regular and a very popular performer at the Thunderbird in the evenings and drew quite a crowd.*
>
> *It is my understanding that if there was any carnal sin in Jacksonville in that time period, there's a good chance the Thunderbird might somehow be involved. It was discreetly over the bridge and away from the prying eyes of the downtown and Riverside/Avondale crowd, on the leading edge of the wilderness known as Arlington.*

George Henderson, of the Westside, e-mailed me his connection to the Thunderbird:

> *I began working at the Thunderbird Hotel in 1972 when I was 17. I worked as both as a busboy and a waiter in the restaurant. The*

The Zodiac Room at the Thunderbird Motor Hotel. *Courtesy of Donna Stein McNett.*

Hotel was beautiful. The landscape immaculately maintained, the pool water was crystal clear, and all of the rooms were clean with crisp linen. It was the upscale hotel in Jacksonville. The hotel was located on Arlington Expressway and directly behind the Town and Country Shopping center located on University Boulevard. The restaurant itself looked a lot like the restaurants in the old 1940's movies where people in the front of the restaurant would sit around tables with luxurious high back booths eating food and sipping their drinks. We did not have carts to deliver food to our customers. Like in the old movies, we had to carry the food to each table using a tray balanced and held over our head. Once we got to the table, we placed the tray on a little stand. All of the tables faced a music stage.

The Thunderbird management would routinely book musical groups to entertain their customers. During the evening, they would dim the lights and the only lights were the candles on the tables and the stage lights. Some of the acts I can remember were Frankie Laine and the Four Diamonds. I left Jacksonville at the end of 1976 to join the Air Force. I recently returned to Jacksonville and drove by the old Thunderbird. It was closed and all of the fences shut tight. The hotel I knew was no longer recognizable. Somewhere over time it was turned into a conference center and all of the beautiful color was painted over in an ugly beige paint. The magic that was once the Thunderbird had long departed.

The glory days of such venues as the Thunderbird are long past, it would seem. And who knows why such wonderful places fall out of fashion. Still, Jacksonville can be proud that we once had this sophisticated place that big-name entertainers would care to visit and that we could enjoy in style.

ANNIE TIQUES

On Wednesday, September 12, 1973, the *Florida Times-Union* ran a story with a headline that read, "Newcomer to City's Restaurant Circles/Annie's Old Fashion Type." Cynthia Parks wrote that "two Tennessee fellers have come to town to show the flatlanders how to enjoy steaks. It should be done by the light of Tiffany-style lamps, surrounded by brass spittoons, slot machines, barber poles and other artifacts of the Rampant Nostalgia Era, which is the mark of the 70s among young swingers."

Carl Kantor and Mike Mason opened their new restaurant Annie Tiques at Regency Square on September 21. The owner of Regency Square had wanted a restaurant/bar in the tradition of New York's TGI Fridays, and since Kantor and Mason had run a TGI Fridays in Tennessee for more than two years, they fit the bill. They took over a former restaurant site in the mall and opened their new business with an original name.

Parks also said in her article that Kantor and Mason collected all manner of antiques from Tennessee and even from a Jacksonville synagogue and came up with a "motley assortment" that will make "live entertainment unnecessary."

One person who was there to witness this grand beginning of something really "hip" was John Butterbrodt, retired teacher now living on a five-acre tract on a mountain in Tennessee. For a poor kid from New Jersey, helping to open the new Annie Tiques in Jacksonville, Florida, was "a blast." In September 1973, Butterbrodt found himself working in a new world surrounded by antiques and restaurant paraphernalia so that he could put himself through college. He wasn't complaining by any means. "I was

Left: Sandalwood's Girl Choral Ensemble, image found in the 1977 *Sandscript*, the Sandalwood Senior High School yearbook. *Courtesy of Patsy Groth Butterbrodt.*

Below: The Soulful Saints, found in the 1977 *Sandscript. Courtesy of Patsy Groth Butterbrodt.*

Above: The Rock Girls, found in the 1977 *Sandscript*. *Courtesy of Patsy Groth Butterbrodt.*

Left: Annie Tiques matchbook. *Courtesy of Claire Fleming King.*

getting $100 to $300 a night working there as a server. Some nights were not quite this good, but Thursdays, Fridays and Saturdays were great."

John talked with great affection about Annie Tiques and what it was like to open a new restaurant. It was exciting and exhausting, and it made his college career possible. He even became so adept at opening restaurants that he began specializing in openings and was eventually sought out to open several other places.

One of the best memories he has of the Annie Tiques was Thursday nights. "We always did a gangbuster business on that night. It was TGIF when we welcomed in that week's Friday. At 10:00 p.m., after the dinner hours were over, we removed all the tables from the center, and the place would go wild. Drinks and appetizers were served, and then there was dancing."

Alvin Brown, a former Jacksonville resident, also had memories of Annie Tiques. "Annie Tiques was another place we went to regularly. It was at Regency Square, which was the closest (and at the time, best) mall at that time. The stained-glass lamps and accents predated Fridays and was a fun place to go and eat."

Cheryl Berlin, who was at the time an Arlington resident, said:

Annie Tiques was at Regency Square next to a tux rental place (not in the mall). It was the happening place to be on Thursday nights! Whirlybird would make a visit, and you never knew what his entrance would be. One time he made a parachute landing in the parking lot—hilarious!

My sister, Debbie, was meeting a guy friend of hers at Annie Tiques on October 13, 1973. I had heard about this new place and what a fun place it was to be. My sister asked me to join them, and I decided to go along. We were sitting at the bar, and if you ever went there, you'll remember the big wooden elephant at the front of the restaurant and the beautiful bar. While we were sitting there, I noticed this cute bartender. He was quite the entertainer, flipping bottles and ringing the bell when a "good tip" was given to the bartender(s). I quietly told my sister that he was really cute. She must have told her friend what I said, and somehow this statement was conveyed to the cute bartender.

Cheryl eventually revealed that she and this bartender celebrated their thirty-ninth wedding anniversary in March 2013. They have three children and three grandchildren. For Cheryl, Annie Tiques proved to be quite special, but the rest of us were simply happy celebrating the advent of the weekend in a cool, hip place that served great food and provided fun times.

Conclusion

In the summer of 2013, there were 1,181 eating establishments in the Jacksonville area—at least, according to *The Real Yellow Pages for 2013–2014*, the only phonebook I get anymore. The number of 2013 restaurants is almost triple the number of those of 1960, a scant fifty-three years ago.

Our population has almost doubled since then, as well. The 1960 U.S. Census as recorded on the University of Central Florida Libraries online site noted that Duval County had a population of 455,411 in 1960. By 2010, the U.S. Census Bureau's online site had Jacksonville's population at 821,784. It would stand to reason that Jacksonville needed more restaurants as it grew, and if I am hearing the pundits correctly, this generation of Americans is eating out far more than earlier generations did. Naturally, restaurants have come into being to meet the demand.

Sadly, as I look back at all the restaurants there were in our area, I admit that my book has left out far too many wonderful places. I can just hear people asking, "What about the Charcoal Steak House or the Tree Steak House in Arlington or Begal's or the Derby House?" And "What about the Bombay Bicycle Club or the Steak & Ale or Victoria Station or Pullman Pies? Where are the pizza parlors like Nick's Pizza, Angelo's or Pizza by Pizzaro?"

Jennifer Cochley Robinson, who lives in Mandarin, is certain to wonder why I cut that chapter on pizza as I approached my deadline. She wasn't fond of pizza as a kid since the only pizza she had ever had came from a Chef Boyardee box. Thankfully, she discovered Pizza by Pizzaro and a whole new taste sensation.

I left out the sandwich shops, like Stand 'n' Snack and Dan's, and I had no place for all the fabulous ice cream parlors like the Westside's Dreamette (although it seems to have come back to life in Mandarin) and Dipper Dan's.

There is no Lums. No drugstore dinettes or soda fountains. No Hasty Tasty and no Tasty Toasty. Amber House and the Toll House are not here, and Uncle John's Pancakes and Uncle Joe's are not either.

There are some restaurants that feel as if they should be covered in this book not because they go so far back in our collective history, but because they have never been "lost"—they really didn't belong. For decades, they have been serving the Jacksonville community: Cotton's Barbeque, Beach Road Chicken Dinners, Bono's, Chopstick Charley's, Jenkins's Barbeque, Sorrento's Italian Restaurant and the Alhambra Dinner Theater. These are most special sites and should be revered because these restaurants have overcome the ebbs and flow of economies, fires, changes of ownership and traffic-flow issues. They have found the secret to long restaurant life and are still open for business today.

I apologize to all those who find that their favorite restaurants did not make it into this effort. In my defense, there were so many, but I covered the restaurants that were mentioned most often. The restaurants in this book are the ones that seemed to resonate the most passionately with those I interviewed and polled.

As I come to the end of this project, I am overcome with a bittersweet sensation—I am glad to be nearing the end of this research work, but I am also sad to be placing these iconic pieces of history back on the shelf of my memory. Researching them, interviewing their owners and patrons and talking about them with friends, old and new, almost made them live again. I could see each dining room as people described it and told me their stories. I could hear restaurant sounds and smell the wonderful aromas as special dishes were detailed. I was also privy to the secret happenings in kitchens and offices, and that was such a tremendous honor.

The time has come for me to turn off the computer, put on my best dress and head out to new Jacksonville restaurants. Even the "lost restaurants" were new once. Perhaps I can make a few more dining memories that will warm me in years to come. And who knows—maybe there will be another book in the offing as I make the restaurant rounds.

Bon appétit!

Bibliography

City of Jacksonville. "Installation of Lee Adams' Mural, 'Ribault's Landing.'" May 1, 2012. http://www.coj.net/commemorate450/events/all-events/installation-of-lee-adams--mural,--ribault-s-landi.aspx.

Edwards, Elizabeth. *Saving Graces: Finding Solace and Strength from Friends and Strangers.* New York: Broadway Books, 2006.

Florida Times-Union Microfilm collection. Second floor, Jacksonville Public Library, downtown Jacksonville, Florida.

Phelps, Joyce. "Silver Spoon." *Jacksonville Journal*, October 28, 1988.

Robertson, Charles. *Witness Protection.* Acoustic Music Production and Sound Pros., 2002. CD.

Tarr, Rodger L. *Hemingway Review* 25, no. 2 (Spring).

Tarr, Rodger L., ed. *Max and Marjorie: The Correspondence between Maxwell E. Perkins and Marjorie Kennan Rawlings.* Gainesville: University of Florida Press, 1999.

YouTube. "Vintage Florida Films—1942—Part One." Published by KailuaKid, November 8, 2012. http://www.youtube.com/watch?v=qGzS-AbE7A0.

INTERVIEWS

Adeeb, Barry. Personal interview with author, April 2, 2013.

Berlin, Cheryl. E-mail interview with author, June 3, 2013.

Brown, Alvin. E-mail interview with author, May 27, 2013.

Butterbrodt, John. Telephone interview with author, August 7, 2013.

Butterbrodt, Patsy. Telephone interview with author, August 7, 2013.

Curtis, Lynn. Telephone interview with author, August 6, 2013.

Eaton, D.H. Telephone interview with author, May 22, 2013.

Eyrick, Ivy Ludwig. Telephone interview with author, July 29, 2013.

Fages, Sheldon. E-mail interview with author, May 28, 2013.

Gallun, Kathy O'Leary. E-mail interview with author, June 2, 2013.

Glassman, Jan. E-mail interview with author, May 27, 2013.

Gordon, Larry. Personal interview with author, August 11, 2013.

Henderson, George. E-mail interview with author, May 23, 2013.

Hill, John. Telephone interview with author, July 24, 2013.

Jennette, Art. Personal interview with author, July 11, 2013.

Johansen, Nina Hazelhurst. Personal interview with author, May 6, 2013.

Kalkines, Christopher. E-mail interview with author, May 29, 2013.

Kouvaris, Sam. Personal interview with author, August 1, 2013.

Manuel, Kenneth. Personal interview with author, April 24, 2013.

Marvin, Kathy Johansen. Personal interview with author, May 6, 2013.

McNett, Donna Stein. E-mail interview with author, May 28, 2013.

Nordan, Gene. Personal interview with author, March 15, 2013.

Reddick, Barbara Manuel. Personal interview with author, April 24, 2013.

Rhodes, Kathy Kalkines. Telephone interview with author, May 27, 2013.

Robertson, Charles. Telephone interview with author, May 31, 2013.

Ross, Buddy. Telephone interview with author, June 5, 2013.

Strickland, Michael. Personal interview with author, July 30, 2013.

Thomas, John. Personal interview with author, July 16, 2013.

Wannamaker, Jennifer. Personal interview with author, August 11, 2013.

Index

S

Sears, Roebuck & Company 14
Sea Turtle 20, 74, 75, 78, 79, 80, 92,
    96
Seitz, David 64
Seligman, Gus 26
Smotherman, Helen 30
Smotherman, Mrs. Ted 30
Smotherman, Roger 30
Some Place Else 56, 57, 58, 59
Steer Room 19, 20, 21, 42, 82
Stein, Albert 110
Stein, David 110
Stein, Martin 110
Stratton, Dick 41, 51
Strickland, B.J. "Uncle Ben" 67
Strickland, Michael 65, 67, 68
Strickland's Seafood 65, 67, 69
Strickland's Town House 67, 68, 69
Strickland, W.F. 67
Surfside 6 57, 62

T

Tallichet, David C., Jr. 61
Texas Drive Inn 84
Thomas, John 50
Thunderbird Motor Hotel 110

W

Wachholz, Pat 59
Waldz 30
Walters, Stuart 32
Worman, Morris 31
Worman's 30, 31
Worman, Sam 30, 31, 33

Y

Yano, Bill 40
Yano, Takatoshi 38, 40

About the Author

D orothy Fletcher, a longtime resident of Jacksonville, graduated from Florida State University in 1972, taught high school English for thirty-five years in the Duval County School System and has had five books published. She has won many poetry contests and has published in many literary journals and magazines. She loves traveling the world with her husband, Hardy, now that they have retired from teaching. She considers being with her grandchildren to be her greatest job.